Escaping the Governance Trap

"For over a century, the United States has learned, forgotten, and painfully relearned that the troubles and trials of Central America flow north. Neil Shenai's *Escaping the Governance Trap* offers practical economic, political, social, and institutional steps to help El Salvador, Guatemala, and Honduras build security and hope. Shenai combines scholarly research with a practitioner's feel for sequencing, integrating diverse activities, building support, accepting the imperfect, and showing results—all with the fundamental ingredients of patience and persistence. Those who speak of the 'root causes' of the woes of the Northern Triangle need the ideas in this book."

—Robert B. Zoellick, *Former President of the World Bank Group, United States Trade Representative, United States Deputy Secretary of State, and author of* America in the World: A History of US Diplomacy and Foreign Policy

"Neil Shenai's *Escaping the Governance Trap* is an edifying read for policymakers and emerging-markets investors. This book presents a vital perspective on how to analyze and address structural development issues arising from a lack of governing capacity in the Northern Triangle, with lessons applicable to many other developing nations. Shenai's accessible prose deftly draws on established theories while positing his own novel viewpoint. Notably, the book provides refreshingly clear-eyed prescriptions to support growth and sociopolitical stability in a strategically important region in need of pragmatic policy interventions."

—Tara Hariharan, *Managing Director of Global Macro Research at NWI Management L.P., member of the Inter-American Dialogue, 2022 Economic Club of New York Fellow, and Term Member of the Council on Foreign Relations*

"Neil Shenai's book, *Escaping the Governance Trap*, is a valuable examination of how the United States and others can help address the 'root causes' of migration from Central America. Shenai argues convincingly how sustained economic reforms should be essential tools in helping the 'Northern Triangle' countries, Guatemala, El Salvador, and Honduras, to escape the debilitating 'governance trap,' which has so long hindered substantial progress in these three countries and fuels the massive outflow of migrants heading to the United States. Shenai persuasively describes how the United States and other 'stakeholders' should be prepared for a long and challenging path to bring about the needed changes in these countries. He explains why the investment to help transform these 'imperfect' partners is in the strategic interests of the United States and others in the region. Of special value, Shenai shares 10 solid principles that can help guide the United States and others in this work of transforming the realities in the Northern Triangle. This book is a thoughtful and helpful contribution as the United States strives to forge enduring solutions to the large northward flows of migrants from Central America."

—Earl Anthony (Tony) Wayne, *Career Ambassador (ret.), United States Foreign Service, Distinguished Diplomat in Residence, School of International Service, American University and Advisory Board Co-Chair, Mexico Institute, Woodrow Wilson Center*

"Central America's Northern Triangle is the source of an endless flow of migrants and subject to demonization for its corrupt politicians and brutal gangs. There is much less serious debate about what policy changes and reforms could bring the region out of cycles of violence and poverty. Neil Shenai's *Escaping the Governance Trap* is a great contribution to the debate with its sharp observations and concrete proposals for change in the region's economic governance. It has the potential of being a much-needed start of a broad debate about the 'root causes' and solutions to Central America's many challenges."

—Benedicte Bull, *Professor of Political Science, Centre for Development and the Environment (SUM), University of Oslo*

"In *Escaping the Governance Trap*, Neil Shenai offers path-breaking solutions to the path-dependent problems of governance in the Northern Triangle of Central America. While the weaknesses of Central American states might appear locked-into domestic submission to powerful elites and international submission to powerful neighbors, opportunities for an alternative equilibrium exist. Shenai offers a set of fiscal, monetary, financial, and macroeconomic reforms chosen not only for their economic impact, but especially for their potential to contribute to democratic state capacity—the ability of the state to penetrate society and provide order and development without descending into autocracy. Of critical importance is the role of external actors, especially the United States government and private sector, which can contribute to path-breaking, rather than path-dependence, when it comes to state capacity in El Salvador, Guatemala, and Honduras."

—Aaron Schneider, *Leo Block Professor of International Studies at the University of Denver and author of* State-Building and Tax Regimes in Central America

Neil Shenai

Escaping the Governance Trap

Economic Reform in the Northern Triangle

palgrave
macmillan

Neil Shenai
Washington, DC, USA

ISBN 978-3-030-99022-0 ISBN 978-3-030-99023-7 (eBook)
https://doi.org/10.1007/978-3-030-99023-7

This Palgrave Pivot imprint is published by the registered company Springer Nature Switzerland AG
The registered company address is: Gewerbestrasse 11, 6330 Cham, Switzerland

To Daphne, Teddy, and Pippa

Foreword

Most anyone trying to solve the problems of Central America's "Northern Triangle" will encounter one of two obstacles: paralyzing cynicism or its opposite, the temptation to address all of the region's challenges at the same time. Both are understandable responses. El Salvador, Guatemala, and Honduras are poor and have poor growth prospects, held back by small domestic markets, modest natural resources, and a plague of violence and extortion that frighten away even the most intrepid investors. Things were looking up in the 1990s, after El Salvador and Guatemala emerged from prolonged and bloody civil conflicts. In recent years, however, the region's leaders have rarely inspired optimism. Homicidal gangs and other criminal actors run roughshod over public authorities. Meanwhile, climate change haunts farmers, as hurricanes and drought leave many hungry and millions willing to leave for a chance at a better life. Scholars could be forgiven for throwing in the towel. Others throw the kitchen sink. Central America needs better schools and better hospitals, better roads and better ports, better police and better politicians. Their lists are dauntingly long, prohibitively costly for both governments and donors, and defy prioritization.

Neil Shenai's *Escaping the Governance Trap: Economic Reform in the Northern Triangle* sidesteps both of these landmines. This book is clear-eyed about the region's challenges but not defeatist. Refreshingly, Shenai is parsimonious and practical in his policy advice.

The Northern Triangle countries offer manufacturers relatively low wages, and proximity and largely tariff-free access to the world's largest economy. Neighboring Panama and Costa Rica showcase the region's transshipment and logistics potential; opportunities for "near shoring" factories from East Asia; and the capacity to draw tourists to Central America's stunning beaches and biodiversity. U.S. missionaries, aid workers, and Peace Corps volunteers who roam the Northern Triangle return home with Honduran Lenca pottery, Guatemalan coffee beans, and a mission to find the best Salvadoran *pupusas* north of the border. Yet the Northern Triangle countries keep bumping up against an economic development ceiling. Shenai has given that ceiling a name, the "governance trap." On paper, the region's governments look like any other. But their security services are outgunned by criminal organizations. Their ministries of education, health, and transportation fail to deliver basic services. Corruption drains limited public resources and allows business executives and crime bosses to puppeteer regulators and elected officials. Shenai simultaneously pins this "path-dependent equilibrium" on government overreach—such as in the management of unproductive state-owned enterprises—and state absence, including the region's underdeveloped approaches to combat money laundering.

Fortunately, *Escaping the Governance Trap* offers a path to a better equilibrium, or for "getting to Denmark," as development scholars like to say. Many of the region's problems are a consequence of cash-strapped governments, starved by tax evasion and poorly designed tax systems. Most notorious is Guatemala, where almost three-quarters of wage earners do not pay any personal income tax. Boosting public revenues would permit Northern Triangle governments to fight poverty and guarantee decent health care, education, and infrastructure. As Shenai tells it, sustained fiscal reforms, complemented by improved debt management, greater financial inclusion (and less financial crime), and productivity-enhancing structural reforms bolstered by generous and consistent support from the United States and other international partners, would unlock the region's growth potential and power the first steps toward economic convergence.

Shenai, who earned his Ph.D. from the Johns Hopkins University School of Advanced International Studies and cut his teeth at the United States Treasury, is a classic scholar-practitioner. His diagnoses and cures reflect both the best ideas from experts on good governance and lessons learned from the school of hard knocks—in this case, the repeated attempts by the U.S. government to bring security, stability, and prosperity to these troubled lands. During Barack Obama's first term, I was responsible for Honduras policy at the State Department when the Central America Regional Security Initiative sought to fix the Northern Triangle's troubles. In President Obama's second term, the White House launched the Alliance for Prosperity in the Northern Triangle—an initiative I observed first-hand as a Director on the White House's National Security Council staff. Donald Trump designed a strategy focused on private investment and border security. None, unfortunately, brought lasting change. Today, as the Joseph Biden administration considers its own $4 billion experiment, *Escaping the Governance Trap* offers an invaluable, back-to-the-basics framework.

The stakes could not be higher. That is principally true for the millions of Salvadorans, Guatemalans, and Hondurans struggling to protect their families and *llegar a fin de mes* (or "to make ends meet"). But the U.S. interest in solving the Northern Triangle's "governance trap" is also compelling. The crush of migrants at the U.S. Southwest border is now a permanent logistical and political crisis, and El Salvador, Guatemala, and Honduras still account for the lion's share of the caravans that are overwhelming the U.S. migration system. As anyone who has worked on policy reform in the Northern Triangle knows, there is often a misalignment between the ambitions of Washington and the political will in Guatemala City, San Salvador, and Tegucigalpa. Moreover, the attention span in the U.S. government is as capricious as its foreign aid budget. Given the scale of Central America's problems and their undeniable impact on the United States, however, dramatic policy fixes will someday be in demand. Shenai writes of "windows of opportunity" for transformational reform. Thanks to this book, when the next one opens, we will now know where to begin.

Washington, DC, USA — Benjamin N. Gedan, Ph.D.

Preface

From 2016 to 2018, I served as the United States Treasury's Financial Attaché to Mexico and Central America based in Mexico City. It was a rewarding job that involved following on-the-ground developments in the region, building relationships with public and private sector contacts, and sending timely updates to my colleagues back in Washington, DC. Given the United States' focus on migration, my headquarters often sent me to the Northern Triangle countries of El Salvador, Guatemala, and Honduras. While in country, I would meet with the region's finance ministries and central banks, checkered with lunches, roundtable discussions, and one-off meetings with diplomats, financiers, business people, politicians, and other key economic actors. I found my counterparts to be generally pragmatic. They knew their countries faced challenges and wanted to solve them, often taking career risks to do so. Their problems, which to some seemed intractable and devoid of immediate solutions, were compounded by trying to navigate the whims of United States policy toward the region. Through my visits, I realized that there was a gap in popular narratives about the Northern Triangle and the on-the-ground reality.

Upon returning to the United States, I wanted to write a book to help academics and policymakers better understand the Northern Triangle and to provide an actionable guide to economic reforms in the region. The premise of *Escaping the Governance Trap: Economic Reform in the Northern Triangle* is that the Northern Triangle's economic problems, including fiscal challenges, impunity, informality, insecurity, and weak growth, stem from governance vulnerabilities. I describe this condition as the *governance trap*, which is defined as *a path-dependent equilibrium in which weak states with contested authority fail to penetrate civil society and achieve self-sustaining economic growth, resulting in states that under supply political order and economic opportunity*. Addressing any symptom of the region's problems, such as poverty and insecurity, requires understanding their shared root causes, which I believe is governance weakness. Given this reality, lasting change in the Northern Triangle requires addressing governance trap conditions, including through economic reforms. The reforms I present in this book thus seek to strengthen public sector accountability, increase fiscal space and resilience, safeguard macroeconomic sustainability, improve financial access and deterrence, and boost potential growth. My recommendations exclude many areas of institutional weakness, from the low quality of the region's education to the inadequacy of its infrastructure. These omissions admittedly reflect a bias for my areas of expertise but also my belief that a series of economic reforms could unlock solutions to a range of governance challenges, with positive spillovers to other areas of institutional weakness. While I believe the Northern Triangle countries can change their trajectories, this book is not blindly optimistic. The Northern Triangle countries will not address their governance challenges overnight and on their own. What is needed is a patient and sustained approach by international partners to support reforms in the region, even if these efforts do not yield immediate results. Escaping the governance trap is a generational project. It is my hope that when conditions allow, the ideas I present will be useful for reformers with a stake in the future of the Northern Triangle. Until the Northern Triangle countries escape the governance trap, droves of their citizens will try to escape their governance traps through continued irregular migration.

Finally, the views expressed in this book are mine alone and do not represent those of any government, international organization, or any other entity mentioned herein.

Washington, DC, USA

Neil Shenai

Acknowledgements

I thank my colleagues, mentors, and friends who helped me write this book, including Alex Acosta, Scott Alvarez, Robert Baldwin, Sascha Buetzer, Benedicte Bull, Zachary Cafritz, Emmanuel Comolet, Jannick Damgaard, Sam duPont, Shereef Elnahal, Ramon Escobar, Kate Eyerman, Jeff Fabre, Rick Farber, Francisca Fernando, Tara Hariharan, Eddie Haubrich, Theodore Kahn, Trevor Kellogg, Tobias Krahnke, Peter Lee, Jane Lesslie, Herschel Nachlis, Joseph Palombo, Arturo Porzecanski, Shyla Raghav, Benjamin Rankin, Dan Raviv, Jon Raviv, Mark Rosen, Aaron Schneider, Arthur Sode, David Steinberg, Eduardo Suarez, Kyle Thomson, David Vannier, Tony Wayne, Jeremy Weil, Alex Zerden, and Robert Zoellick. I especially thank Benjamin Gedan for lending me his deep insight into Latin America, commenting on my draft chapters, and graciously writing this book's foreword. I am deeply indebted to the late Daniel Moger, my friend and former U.S. Treasury colleague, for sending me to Mexico and giving me the professional opportunity of a lifetime. May he rest in peace. I thank Tula Weis at Palgrave Macmillan for her patient stewardship of this project from my initial proposal, through a few reformulations, to this finished book. I also appreciate the candid feedback from my anonymous peer reviewers, though all remaining errors are mine alone. Writing this book was possible because of the love and support of my family. I thank my parents, Shaila Shenai and Kamalakar Shenai, for making immense personal sacrifices to immigrate to the

United States. Thanks to my sister, Radhika, for her regular visits to Washington and encouragement. I thank my wife, Daphne, our family's Latin Americanist, for urging me to study governance seriously and for shouldering the burden of pandemic-era parenting as I finished this book. My son Teddy and daughter Pippa, who was born as this manuscript went into production, helped too by keeping my priorities straight and by imbuing my life with indescribable meaning.

Contents

About the Author

Neil Shenai served as the U.S. Treasury's Financial Attaché to Mexico and Central America from 2016 to 2018. He is a Term Member of the Council on Foreign Relations and author of *Social Finance: Shadow Banking during the Global Financial Crisis* (Palgrave Macmillan, 2018). He received his Ph.D. from Johns Hopkins University School of Advanced International Studies.

Abbreviations

AMEXID	Mexican Agency for International Cooperation and Development
AML	Anti-Money Laundering
BTC	Bitcoin
CAC	Collective-Action Clause
CAFTA-DR	United States-Dominican Republic-Central America Trade Agreement
CAT	Catastrophe Bond
CBDC	Central Bank Digital Currency
CFATF	Caribbean Financial Action Task Force
CFT	Combating the Financing of Terrorism
CIA	Central Intelligence Agency
CICIES	International Commission against Corruption and Impunity in El Salvador
CICIG	International Commission Against Impunity in Guatemala
DLT	Distributed Ledger Technology
DNFBP	Designated Non-Financial Business and Professions
ECLAC	United Nations Economic Commission for Latin America and the Caribbean
ENEE	*Empresa Nacional de Energía Eléctrica*
FATF	Financial Action Task Force
FDI	Foreign Direct Investment
FIU	Financial Intelligence Unit
FMLN	Farabundo Martí National Liberation Front
GAFILAT	Financial Action Task Force of Latin America
GDP	Gross Domestic Product
IFI	International financial institution

IMF	International Monetary Fund
KYC	Know Your Customer
M2	U.S. M2 Money Supply
MACCIH	Mission in Support of the Fight against Corruption and Impunity in Honduras
MS-13	*Mara Salvatrucha*
NAFTA	North American Free Trade Agreement
NIC	Newly Industrialized Country
OAS	Organization of American States
PPP	Purchasing Power Parity
SCDI	State-Contingent Debt Instrument
SDRM	Sovereign Debt Restructuring Mechanism
TCO	Transnational Criminal Organization
UIRP	Uncovered Interest Rate Parity
VAT	Value-Added Tax

List of Figures

Chapter 1

Chapter 2

List of Tables

CHAPTER 1

From the Northern Triangle to Northern Europe: How Good Governance Can Rescue Central America

Abstract The Northern Triangle countries of El Salvador, Guatemala, and Honduras are stuck in "governance traps" in which economic informality, violence and insecurity, state capture and corruption, and a lack of state capacity limit their ability to meet the needs of their populations. The governance trap is defined as a path-dependent equilibrium in which weak states with contested authority fail to penetrate civil society and achieve self-sustaining economic growth, resulting in states that under supply political order and economic opportunity. This governance trap framework rests on several propositions. First, the state is an autonomous organization that has a monopoly over the legitimate use of force in a given territory. Second, the Northern Triangle countries have weak states due to their contested monopoly of violence and thus, improving their governance will require improving their Weberian stateness. Third, state capacity is a composite of the mix of activities pursued by the Northern Triangle countries (their "scope") and their ability to penetrate civil society autonomously (their "strength"). Fourth, some strength-scope combinations are better geared toward promoting high-quality governance than others. Fifth, because institutions exhibit path dependence, successful reforms will likely require strong, multi-year long commitments. Sixth, it is possible to "get to Denmark" with the right set of reforms, political will, and timely help from international partners.

N. Shenai, *Escaping the Governance Trap*,
https://doi.org/10.1007/978-3-030-99023-7_1

Keywords Getting to Denmark · Governance trap · Max Weber · Northern Triangle economic reform · Path dependence

During the 2010s, millions of citizens from the Northern Triangle countries of El Salvador, Guatemala, and Honduras left their homes for a chance to enter the United States.[1] Why do so many people leave?

In short, life in the Northern Triangle is tough. Conditions are comparable to "war zones," insofar as "murder, kidnappings, threats, recruitment by non-state armed actors, extortion, sexual violence, and forced disappearance" are part of everyday life, according to Doctors Without Borders (Doctors Without Borders, 2017, 6). Homicide rates remain well above global averages.

Insecurity contributes to tepid economic performance. Northern Triangle poverty rates exceed those of their neighboring states. Tepid economic growth and anemic job creation push workers into the informal sector, depriving the Northern Triangle governments of tax revenue. TCOs and gangs capitalize on the Northern Triangle's weak states, security vacuums, and corruption to extract rents from firms and individuals, asphyxiating small businesses and discouraging investment. Starved of revenue and jousting for influence with TCOs, governments cannot incentivize productive economic activity. Infrastructure investment, social spending, and other high-multiplier expenditures are foregone, while low tax bases reduce the resilience of the Northern Triangle to adverse events.

[1] To make it to the United States, irregular migrants must avoid being caught by immigration authorities or seek out one of the few legal migration pathways for low-skilled individuals. They must also avoid non-state transnational criminal organizations (TCOs) and local smugglers that view migrants as opportunities of exploitation and profit. For instance, migrants report being subjected to forced prostitution, kidnapping, and being separated from their families for months while transiting from the Northern Triangle to the United States (International Crisis Group, 2017). A United Nations study found that several migrant women reported bringing birth control in transit to avoid being impregnated by rapists during their trips (UNHCR, 2015, 44). Also, taking the trip often costs one's life savings or borrowing at usurious interest rates. Janetsky and Stunt find that Guatemalan migrants pay interest rates of more than twenty-five percent to borrow funds for their trips to the United States (Janetsky & Stunt, 2020).

The Northern Triangle countries suffer from unfavorable geography. They are susceptible to climate-related shocks, including droughts and hurricanes, and are vulnerable to earthquakes and volcano eruptions. Their rugged terrain makes it difficult to build economic interconnections and regional value chains, denying these small economies the necessary scale to take economic advantage of their proximity to the United States (Meyer & Taft-Morales, 2019). Their location between drug producing countries in South America and the drug consuming United States make them the site of violent turf battles as TCOs seek to dominate the region's drug corridor and extract revenues from this multi-billion-dollar market (Meyer, 2019). The drug trade also fuels high-level corruption and undermines the rule of law. Meanwhile, gangs such as MS-13 extort local businesses (Plotnikov, 2019).

The COVID-19 pandemic, ongoing structural shifts in the global economy, and the global climate emergency further complicate the prospects for growth, posing a generational health, economic, and socio-political challenges for the region.

The scale of these challenges and their systemic effects—in addition to their impact on the lives of tens of millions of Guatemalans, Hondurans, and Salvadorans—underscore the need to understand the problems facing the Northern Triangle and what can be done about them. The Northern Triangle's proximity to the United States means that local problems in the Northern Triangle can balloon into systemically important crises in the United States related to border security and immigration policy. In turn, the actions of the United States, influenced in part by Northern Triangle migration, can trigger drastic policy challenges for the global system, including for some of the United States' closest allies and partners.

The purpose of this book is three-fold:

First, *Escaping the Governance Trap* provides a framework for thinking about the Northern Triangle's challenges, arguing that the lack of *governing capacity* in all three Northern Triangle countries is a crucial problem. These countries are stuck in "governance traps," which is defined as a *path-dependent equilibrium in which weak states with contested authority fail to penetrate civil society and achieve self-sustaining economic growth, resulting in states that under supply political order and economic opportunity*. This framework emerges from several academic literatures related to political order and the role of the state, institutional economics, and economic and political development theory. This chapter summarizes the foundational theoretical propositions on which this book's governance trap framework rests and explains this framework in the context of the Northern Triangle.[2]

Second, Chapter 2 makes the case that economic reforms can help the Northern Triangle countries escape their governance traps. It argues that economic reforms related to fiscal policy, monetary and exchange rate policy, financial sector policy, and structural reform can help the Northern Triangle enhance their macroeconomic sustainability, invest in their populations, deter illicit activity while expanding financial access, and increase potential growth. These economic reforms have the potential to address each country's governance trap conditions and thus relax the constraints on improving state capacity, political order, and economic growth over time.[3]

Third, Chapter 3 focuses on how international partners such as the United States, Canada, Mexico, civil society, the private sector, and international institutions can help the Northern Triangle countries escape their governance traps. Emphasis is placed on the United States' history of engagement in Latin America, its strategic interests, and principles of engagement that follow from these interests. This chapter argues that sustained international and domestic political will is necessary to push for durable reforms due to the path-dependent (or "trapping") nature of the region's governance problems. Several principles of engagement discussed in Chapter 3 include: foreign stakeholders should be prepared for reform breakthroughs but be realistic about the windows of opportunity for reform. They should be willing to engage imperfect partners when interests coincide while

[2] This book's literature review is not exhaustive, nor does this book argue that the governance trap is a mutually exclusive paradigm for understanding the Northern Triangle. Rather, this book argues that the governance trap framework is a plausible diagnosis of the region's challenges.

[3] Note that these reforms are not presented as silver bullets to the region's problems. No such playbook exists. Rather, these reforms are offered as a starting point for thinking about helping the Northern Triangle countries make a concerted push to escape the governance trap, recognizing that lasting change will require reforms along multiple axes, including politically, socially, and in the states' international relations.

managing the tradeoff between stability and accountability. The private sector and civil society can be allies in reform efforts. Canada, Mexico, and the United States should attempt to bring the Northern Triangle into the North American community. And international support can be useful in addressing governance vulnerabilities in the Northern Triangle, including through vertical accountability mechanisms and multilateral anti-corruption commissions such as the International Commission against Corruption and Impunity in El Salvador (CICIES), International Commission Against Impunity in Guatemala (CICIG), and Mission in Support of the Fight against Corruption and Impunity in Honduras (MACCIH). The logic of these engagement strategies follows from this chapter and Chapter 2.

1 Perspectives on Stateness, Governance, and Economic Growth: Six Propositions

This chapter now places *Escaping the Governance Trap* within the academic literature and provides the theoretical grounding of this book's governance trap framework. It presents six propositions based on literature related to stateness, governance, and economic performance.

> **Proposition 1**: *The state is an autonomous organization that has a monopoly over the legitimate use of force in a delimited territory.*
> **Proposition 2**: *Weak states have a contested monopoly of force and mixed ability to provide political order to their territory.*

The above definition and implication of "stateness" (propositions 1 and 2, respectively) come from German sociologist Max Weber, who provided this widely accepted description of the state that ties together sanctioned violence in a specific physical space. Weber argued that human beings accept political authority when it follows from three sources: traditional authority, charismatic authority, and legal authority. Traditional authority referred to historic patterns of dominion between landowner and serf, which reflect a socio-economic and socio-political relationship and were typical in feudal society. Traditional authority organizes feudal societies. Charismatic authority described the ability of certain leaders to marshal a "gift of grace" to inspire intense personalistic devotion as the basis of political authority. Fascist leaders Adolf Hitler and Benito

Mussolini are examples of charismatic leaders. Legal authority follows from codified rules that conferred statutory obligations and rights for citizens regarding a political authority. Liberal democracies such as the United States rely on legal authority to underpin their stateness. Although the source of state legitimacy ultimately depends on regime type, the perceived *legitimacy* of dominion was Weber's key explanatory variable for the existence of the state (Weber, 1946).[4]

Why do individuals agree to structures of dominion? To Weber and other state theorists, the development of states reflects a cost-benefit analyses of citizens that seek to avoid a Hobbesian "state of nature," or war of all-against-all in which murder, theft, and lawlessness pervade human interaction. According to Thomas Hobbes, in such a state of nature, there would be "no culture… navigation… instruments of moving; no knowledge of the face of the Earth; no account of time; no Arts; no Letters; no Society; and which is worst of all, continual fear, and danger of violent death; and the life of man [is] solitary, poor, nasty, brutish, and short." Thus, man creates, and obeys, the state to escape anarchy, delegating some power and control in exchange for security in a social contract vis-à-vis the state (Hobbes et al., 1996, 88–90). Although subsequent scholars have disagreed about the ideal type of state (be it absolutist, classically liberal, or a hybrid polity, with their distinct sources and mixes of Weberian authority), the state remains a product of a contract to escape the state of nature.[5]

[4] For a foundational piece on the state as a conceptual variable, see Nettl (1968). For widely cited edited volumes on the role of the state as a conceptual variable, enabler of economic development, and as a custodian of sanctioned violence, see Tilly (1982) and Evans et al. (1985). For a survey of more recent literature, see Leibfried et al. (2015).

[5] For an accessible summary of these debates, see Riley (2013) and Micklethwait and Wooldridge (2014), including sections on Locke and Rousseau. Daniel Deudney problematizes the *degrees* of anarchy by providing a spectrum of "violence interaction capacity," which he describes as "an aggregate of violence proximity and violence density." This definition acknowledges that the breadth and depth of violence interaction capacity (ranging from primitive methods to nuclear weapons) implicates the ideal type of state and its composition at different levels of anarchy (both within and among states). To Deudney, "the main parameters of violence interaction capacity are determined by the [complex] interplay of unchanging geography and the changing technologies of communication, transportation, and destruction, which, in turn, alter the significance of geography." For more, see Deudney (2000, 3–4, 2007).

Michael Mann further develops the Weberian concept of the state by describing the state as a composite of four features: (1) differentiated institutions; (2) centralized decision-making; (3) territorial demarcation; and, (4) a monopoly of rulemaking anchored by a monopoly of force. The ability of the state to penetrate non-state social relationships, including civil society, coupled with the state's despotic power determines the type of polity that will arise. States with high despotic power and low penetration into civil society (or, as Mann describes it, low "infrastructural co-ordination"), take on an "imperial" form, whereas those with high despotic power and high penetration are authoritarian. States with low despotic power and low penetration are "feudal," while states with low despotic power and high penetration are considered "bureaucratic" (in the Weberian sense where state institutions have bureaucratic recruitment based on technocratic skill and merit).[6] Regardless of their form, Mann views the state as "autonomous" and exhibiting a "will to power" as a "socio-spatial organization" rather than simply being an aggregate of its constituent parts (Mann, 1984, 125).

The existence of groups that rival the state for the legitimate use of force—such as in countries with large governance vulnerabilities and power vacuums in which non-state actors like TCOs, gangs, and terrorists thrive—does not invalidate the stateness of the polity. Rather, challenges to state authority imply the existence of *weak states*, where the main organs of the state exist on paper and to an extent in practice: the branches of government, courts, customs and tax authorities, police forces, and the armed services exist, though institutions are contested by challengers that attempt to circumvent, co-opt, or corrupt the state apparatus for private gain.

From the viewpoint of Weber and Mann's definitions of stateness, the Northern Triangle countries should be considered weak states with dimensions of imperial and authoritarian state types (Rotberg, 2010, 3–6).[7] While the Northern Triangle countries have Weberian elements of an impersonal bureaucracy and independent institutions with statutory

[6] On Weberian bureaucracy, see Fukuyama (2013, 348).

[7] As Robert Rotberg explains, "a weak state... can disrupt lives and economic activity by its very weakness and its inability to control violence and the destruction of property." He further adds that states can be weak due to autocratic corruption and a low level of state capacity. Although all three Northern Triangle states exhibit autocratic tendencies and have experienced violent political transitions, including involving foreign intervention during the

authority grounded in the rule of law, numerous non-state actors contest this political, economic, and social authority, with TCOs and gangs competing for influence over the state apparatus. These groups competitively seek to co-opt the state via bribery, corruption, and intimidation.[8] As Benedicte Bull notes, the Northern Triangle states are predominated by elite networks guided by large family group economic and political interests, which in turn provide "predictability in highly volatile contexts." A coterie of elite firms tends to win public contracts and other forms of fiscal largesse, thriving on a lack of public transparency. This fiscal capture makes it easier for elites to evade paying taxes, further weakening institutions. To earn the trust of the population, elites wield clever ideological strategies to mobilize trust public in elite networks.[9] When these methods fail, elite networks use the organs of the state to threaten challengers and otherwise disqualify reformer alternatives to their influence. Globalization has not broken this pattern: Bull finds that elite networks continue to exercise their influence despite the Northern Triangle's openness to the global economy. For instance, multinational corporations must team up with these elite networks to overcome formal and informal constraints on economic activity such as permitting, bargaining with workers, obtaining critical inputs, and getting goods to market (Bull, 2014).[10]

The Northern Triangle states lack the human and financial resources, as well as the necessary political will, to deter and stand up to predatory behavior, further compounding their institutional weakness. This process saps the ability of the Northern Triangle governments to deliver critical public goods to their populaces. Public trust in the state erodes,

twentieth century, state incapacity is likely the proximate cause for their underdevelopment (Rotberg, 2010, 182–185).

[8] Arnson and Olson (2011) provide a helpful volume on organized crime in the Northern Triangle.

[9] Bull cites anti-communism, neoliberalism, and religion as examples of ideological tools employed by elites to perpetuate their influence.

[10] Salvador Marti I Puig and Diego Sanchez-Ancochea claim that elite domination of the politics was followed from the peace settlements of civil conflicts in the 1990s. They argue that the Northern Triangle's quasi-democratic institutions "were the result of a military stalemate and international pressures. For the left, the most desirable outcome of the war would have been a 'revolution…for the right in power, a semi-democratic political regime with limited popular participation was probably the best option available." This ambivalence toward democracy explains the periodic rollbacks of democratic institutions in the Northern Triangle. See Marti i Puig and Sanchez-Ancochea (2014, 9).

Table 1 Measuring corruption in the Northern Triangle

	2010		*2015*		*2020*	
	Score	*Rank*	*Score*	*Rank*	*Score*	*Rank*
El Salvador	36	78	39	72	36	104
Guatemala	32	101	28	123	25	149
Honduras	24	143	31	111	24	157
Mexico	31	105	31	111	31	124
United States	71	22	76	16	67	25

Note Transparency International's Corruption Perception Index is based on 13 underlying surveys and is one of the more popular measures of corruption. Note that a higher score (out of 100) and lower relative rank (out of 180 countries) imply a lower perception of corruption.
Source Transparency International

fueling a brain drain and discouraging potential reformers who might alter the suboptimal equilibrium of weak states and underdevelopment. Perceptions of corruption rise (see Table 1). According to data from the Latin America Public Opinion Project at Vanderbilt University and *Latinobarómetro*, about half of the citizens of the Northern Triangle believe that corruption is generalized across government functionaries. About 30% and 40% of respondents believe "all politicians are corrupt" in El Salvador and Honduras, respectively, while 80% of adults claim to have "little to no" trust in the government (see Table 1) (Latin America Public Opinion Project, 2021; Latinobarómetro, 2021). Without addressing this cycle of state weakness, corruption, and the lack of public trust, it will remain difficult for the Northern Triangle countries to escape their underdevelopment and susceptibility to violence.

This literature also suggests that greater penetration into civil society (i.e., improving infrastructural co-ordination) is a double-edged sword. On one hand, states with low despotic power and high penetration are most likely to provide sound governance without descending into autocracy and repression. On the other hand, states with low despotic power and low penetration are likely to be unable to achieve the breadth and depth necessary to meet the needs of the population. Should some degree of despotic power be accepted if doing so improves infrastructural co-ordination? How do international partners convince a state with high despotic power and low penetration into civil society to strengthen its reach into civil society while at the same time paring back its coercive ability? Is such an aim realistic, given the political incentives of leaders and strength of vested interests? There are no easy answers to these questions. There could be circumstances where moving from imperial to authoritarian structures are an intermediate step toward bureaucratic structures per Mann, while other times, imperial or authoritarian structures could be durable in the long term. This question is especially relevant to the discussion of how international actors can engage the Northern Triangle governments as imperfect partners, which is further discussed in Chapter 3.

> **Proposition 3**: *State capacity is a composite of its scope of activities pursued and coercive ability.*
> **Proposition 4**: *As a corollary, some combinations of state scope and strength are better at promoting high quality governance than others.*

Francis Fukuyama claims that Weber and Hobbes' definitions of the state focused on state strength, or the state's ability to coerce behaviors that would otherwise not occur based on individuals' private decisions. To Fukuyama, state strength relates to the ability of the state to *enforce* its will on its constituents, or its capability "to send someone with a uniform and a gun to force people to comply with the state's laws." In addition to differences in state strength, Fukuyama observed that the *locus of state action* varies. For instance, states in Western Europe play a larger role in the economy compared to the United States, which is reflected in Western Europe's higher share of gross domestic product (GDP). Nevertheless, Western Europe and the United States have equally strong claims on the monopoly of violence within their territories. To Fukuyama, the mix of state activities, or its "scope," is distinct from its coercive ability—i.e., its "strength." Fukuyama defines state *scope* as the "different functions and goals taken on by governments" that vary from "necessary and important" to "desirable" and ultimately to those activities that are potentially "counter-productive or even destructive" (Fukuyama, 2004a, 21–22, 2004b). Juxtaposing state scope and strength yields the Fukuyama's strength–scope matrix, presented in Fig. 1.

Although this book does not make a normative judgment about the optimal size of government and ideal mix of state activity—as such a choice should ideally reflect the socio-political consensus unique to each state—it accepts the conclusion advanced by Fukuyama and others that

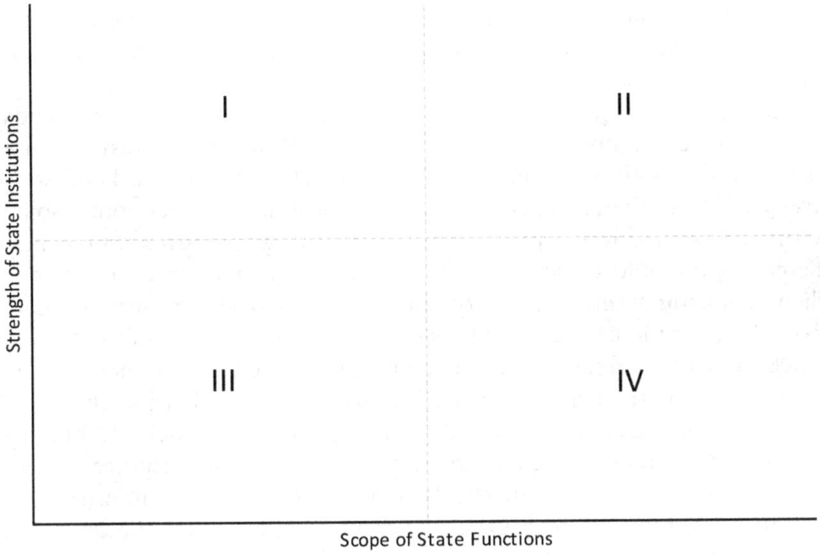

Fig. 1 Fukuyama's matrix of state scope and state strength (*Source* Fukuyama 2004a)

strictly limiting the scope of state activity will not lead to better development outcomes. In fact, delegating parts of the state to the private sector and reducing state capacity in the name of efficiency or to limit opportunities for corruption could be counterproductive to economic development given weak state initial conditions.[11] While much of the focus of this book is the vertical axis of Fukuyama's state strength and scope matrix (see Fig. 1), further consideration should be given to identifying the preferred mix of state scope given initial weak state conditions and the imperative to improve state capacity. For example, state efficacy could be improved by outside stakeholders who, upon receiving political mandates from the Northern Triangle authorities, could deliver critical

[11] This lesson is apt in the Latin American context, where Washington Consensus reforms may have contributed to macroeconomic stability but failed to raise low growth rates in the region, see Goldfajn et al. (2021). Nachlis (2018) further contends that there can develop "pockets of weakness" in otherwise strong institutions, which has theoretical implications for historical institutionalist scholarship (that tend to emphasize state strength) and practical implications on how institutions meet the needs of their clients.

public goods that the Northern Triangle countries are themselves incapable of providing, helping to fill temporary gaps in stateness and thus enhancing governance.

The anti-statist posture of the post-Cold War development agenda should also be reconsidered in the Northern Triangle's context because many of the region's economic challenges stem from a lack of state strength, rather than an overly large state footprint in the economy. Some reforms presented in Chapter 2 require improving state strength (such as increasing the enforcement capacity of Northern Triangle governments' illicit financing fighting capacity), while others relate to altering state scope (such as increasing the state's provision of insurance against climate shocks and other disasters or broadening the state's involvement in the financial sector to increase financial sector access). Balancing improvements to state strength while tailoring state scope is a delicate process that could entrench oligopolistic dynamics and state capture within the economy and polity. In the long run, domestic and international reformers should seek to expand the frontier of potential combinations of stateness and scope, which will better allow the Northern Triangle governments to tailor their activities to the political preferences of their populaces while maintaining their efficacy (see Annex 1).

> **Proposition 5**: *"Bad" institutions and "good" institutions exhibit strongly path-dependent qualities. Thus, initial conditions matter.*

Many political scientists, sociologists, and economists have studied the relationship between institutions and economic performance. One of the key conclusions from these analyses is that institutions—be they productive or predatory—can be self-sustaining in the long term. Douglass North defines an institution as "any form of constraint that human beings devise to shape human interaction." Institutions can be both formal and informal, encompassing codified laws as well as behavioral conventions or norms. They influence economic performance by altering the costs of economic exchange and the incentives for production. Some institutions promote economic activity (such as property rights that allow economic agents to use their assets as collateral to finance productive investment), while other institutions lead to economic stagnation (for instance, when firms have incentives to capture the state to achieve an anti-competitive position in the economy, diverting resources from more productive economic activity, in turn raising prices, and lowering the quality of goods and services) (North, 1990, 4–6).

Once created, institutions perpetuate incentives for agents to maintain those institutions over time. This stickiness is the essence of *institutional path dependence*. To understand path dependence, consider the example of an introduction of a foreign exchange liquidity facility in which a country's central bank provides foreign exchange to key institutions at a discount to the prevailing market exchange rate. Entities with access to the central bank's new foreign exchange window gain a competitive advantage. To maintain this advantage, agents should be willing to spend up to the value of perceived rents in lobbying and other forms of advocacy to maintain access to the favorable foreign exchange rate.[12] As a result, a government may maintain multiple exchange rates into perpetuity even if the initial circumstances that justified the facility changed considerably.

North argues that institutions are path-dependent because a given institutional setup creates conditions for *increasing returns* to the maintenance of those same institutions. Institutions create network externalities by shaping learning effects, organizational behavior, and adaptive expectations within the context of the initial institutional matrix. In this way, institutions bridge previous choices to the constraints from the past (North, 1991). The self-sustaining nature of institutions is agnostic as to whether those institutions produce aggregate welfare-maximizing outcomes—both good and bad institutions are subject to path dependence by shaping the constraints of future behavior.

That institutions can promote and destroy economic growth is not a novel contention. But when do institutions promote economic growth, and when do they immiserate it? Peter Evans differentiated between states that promote economic growth and those that impede it by classifying states on a continuum between *predatory states* and *developmental states*. Predatory states seek to extract economic surplus from the population and provide a low public return on tax revenues and other state resources, reducing the incentives for private actors to accumulate capital. Under

[12] Economists have described the above actions as *rent seeking*, or a situation in which actors seek to acquire rents (or economic surplus in excess of those merited by costs and economically required rates of return) through both legal and illegal means, see Krueger (1974, 2002). The existence of rents creates incentives for agents to divert resources that would otherwise be spent on productive activity (such as capital accumulation) toward extracting rents.

predatory states, those who control the state "seem to plunder without any more regard for the welfare of the citizenry than a predator has for the welfare of its prey." Conversely, some states promote economic growth by shaping incentives for public and private actors to make economically productive choices. These are the "developmental" states, which structure incentives for actors to invest in the future by, for example, mobilizing savings and channeling it to productive investment; safeguarding private gain through property rights and the rule of law; promoting skills acquisition among the workforce; and providing a suite of public and common pool resources that raise the return and lower the risks of these investments. In turn, developmental states promote structural transformation and rising living standards.

Evans compared the experiences of East Asia's newly industrialized countries (NICs) such as Hong Kong, Singapore, South Korea, and Taiwan, with those of Sub-Saharan Africa (including the present-day Democratic Republic of Congo). He concluded that the NICs' distinguishing feature was their "embedded autonomy," in which their governments maintained close ties to private economic actors with delineated responsibilities and a responsiveness to the changing needs of the private sector. Developmental states had Weberian bureaucracies, underpinned by meritocratic recruitment and promotion, with strong technocratic expertise. These developmental states were bureaucratically coherent and provided structure to the commanding heights of the economy, with extensive links to credit provision, labor relations, and a strong bias toward providing key public goods that would help reduce costs and promote development, including by building competitive export sectors (Evans, 1989).

Predatory states, on the other hand, lack bureaucratic coherence and vitiate the ability of private actors to engage in productive economic activity. Predatory states are often dominated by unitary leaders who project power through patronage, rewarding loyalty rather than bureaucratic competence. In predatory states, "personal ties are the only source of cohesion, and individual maximization takes precedence over [the] pursuit of collective goals."

Few states fall cleanly into either of these ideal types and instead exist on a spectrum of embedded autonomy, wherein the state tries to balance several types of involvement in the economy, including enforcement or impeding action (what Evans terms "custodial" action), the production of key outputs ("demiurge"), creating new forms of economic organization and output ("midwivery"), and protecting and guiding economic activity once established ("husbandry"). The ability of a state to promote economic growth depends on its competence and its capacity to strike an appropriate balance among these aims. A state that relies too heavily on custodial enforcement may make it prohibitively expensive to start and sustain a new business, for instance, while too little demiurge would leave an insufficient supply of critical public goods, again making productive private sector activity too costly and thus impossible (Evans, 1995, pp. 11–15). Evans concluded that different types of interventions in the economy, the sensitivity of the state to the needs of the private sector, the strength of the state to channel the self-interests of its private actors, and the existence of an entrepreneurial class of private actors and Weberian bureaucracy help determine a state's development trajectory.[13]

One way of thinking about the path dependence of developmental and predatory states is to consider how they interact with the common structural impediments to broad-based economic growth. Paul Collier argued that about a sixth of humanity is stuck in conditions that prevent achieving lasting economic development. Collier identifies four "traps" that impede development, including the *conflict trap* (in which insecurity and violence prevent economic growth), the *natural resource trap* (which reduces an economy's productive potential due to Dutch disease and rentier effects), the *trap of being landlocked with bad neighbors* (that causes negative spillovers from neighbors and limits trade linkages to the global economy), and the *bad governance in a small country trap.*

[13] The developmental state literature is rich with case studies, often focusing on differences between Sub-Saharan Africa and East Asia, though Latin America's post-World War II development is also often compared to East Asia's. Latin America is often presented as an intermediate case, as Evans describes in the case of Brazil. Prima facie evidence would suggest that the Northern Triangle countries are also intermediate types, with enough embedded autonomy to achieve complex economic tasks (such as pension reform and central banking) but limited state capacity. For a poignant comparison of the development models of India and Korea (with a heavy emphasis on the relative benefits of export-led industrialization compared to import-substitution methods), see Chibber (2003). For additional background on East Asian industrialization, see Wade (1990). For an excellent edited volume, which includes regional perspectives on the developmental state in South Asia and Latin America, see Woo-Cumings (1999). For additional Latin America regional perspectives, see Ferraro and Centeno (2018) and Kurtz (2001) on Chile. For a widely cited literature review on the developmental state, see Öniş (1991).

Collier writes that bad governance can destroy an economy's productive potential, and asserts that governance as a driver of development has asymmetric payoffs: good governance cannot turn around a country with terrible fundamentals, while bad governance can be ruinous. Collier acknowledges that countries can "learn from failure" and improve their trajectories, though lasting interventions are difficult to achieve (Collier, 2007, 3–14, 64–75).

What does this analysis imply for the Northern Triangle's prospects for reform? First, institutions matter to economic development. For this reason, any study of the Northern Triangle's development should examine institutional quality. Second, current conditions could be difficult to escape due to institutional path dependence. Countries can be caught in "traps," such as those associated with weak governance and corruption. Enhancing institutions and moving along the spectrum from predatory to developmental states may require multi-year reform efforts, possibly with the help of external actors. Third, per Collier, good governance is generally a ***necessary but insufficient condition*** to promote economic growth. Improving governance—i.e., what Fukuyama describes as "a government's ability to make and enforce rules" regardless of regime type—can improve the probability of economic development, though it is not a panacea (Fukuyama, 2013). Fourth, countries may have to consider the tradeoffs to balance adequately Evans' different state goals (i.e., finding the right mix of despotic and infrastructural co-ordination powers) while preserving the polity's coherence. This implies that reform efforts should be sensitive to country-specific factors. And fifth, because some members of society, including public and private sector actors, benefit from the status quo, attempts to remove rents and push freed surplus toward productive economic activity should be expected to be difficult and politically contested. Additionally, changing the incentives of elites to align their interests with their broader populaces could reduce the likelihood of vested interests spoiling reform efforts.

Proposition 6: *It is possible to "get to Denmark" with the right policy interventions.*

Lant Pritchett and Michael Woolcock popularized the concept of "Denmark," or a modern state that has achieved both economic and political development. The authors chose Denmark because it has a Weberian bureaucracy in which key public services are provided efficiently by a competent and meritocratic civil service. They acknowledge that there are many paths to get to Denmark and that institutional idiosyncrasies (e.g., the distinction between presidential vs. parliamentary systems) mattered less than overall institutional quality. Pritchett and Woolcock focused on bureaucratic outputs and common malaises that impaired the efficient delivery of public services in their analysis of what it takes to get to Denmark (Pritchett & Woolcock, 2002).

Fukuyama builds on Pritchett and Woolcock's concept of Denmark by arguing that the modern liberal democracy achieves a stable balance between the key institutions of the state, the rule of law, and accountable government. Modern states are necessary but insufficient for getting to Denmark because states can be used for personal ends, such as patronage (i.e., they can be predatory). Thus, the rule of law can serve as a check against the state's excesses. Moreover, accountable governments are those that respond to the needs of their populations. So, to get to Denmark, reformers should focus on improving stateness, the rule of law, and accountability. Although this book does not focus on democratic development per se, as it acknowledges the empirically mixed record of institutional quality and regime type,[14] it accepts the contention made by Fukuyama and others that states that are more responsive to the needs of the public are generally better at public goods provision than less responsive ones; that a minimum level of state strength is necessary for economic development; and that the rule of law is a key determinant of a country's economic climate and thus its attractiveness as a destination for investment and platform of economic development (Fukuyama, 2011, 14–18). It should be emphasized that some aspects of state governance are easier to transfer (or import) than others: organizational design and management is relatively easy to transfer between states, while social or cultural factors tend to be much more persistent and inelastic to outside influence (Fukuyama, 2004b, 31). The challenge for state-building is to

[14] As Fukuyama notes, the empirical record of democracies and autocrats at providing good governance is mixed. Part of the appeal of authoritarian approaches and the ongoing "democratic recession" could relate to the perceived failings of deliberative democracy. Regardless of whether this is a fair or accurate representation, the links between democratic accountability and governance are theoretically straightforward but empirically convoluted, especially with regard to the democratic transition. For more, see Fukuyama (2011, 2013) and Fukuyama and McFaul (2007).

identify the appropriate sequence of reforms and to balance longer-term imperatives (such as altering incentives for the basis of state legitimation and the professionalization of the civil service) with the low-hanging fruit of organizational design. Foreign stakeholders should recognize that changing the laws does not necessarily lead to stronger infrastructural coordination within the polity to honor and implement those laws. The non-transferability of social and cultural factors could be one explanation for the persistence of underdevelopment even in cases where institutional design has improved.

Economists too argue that economic development and catch-up are possible. Much of modern-day development theory is based on the idea of *economic convergence*, which posits that lower-income countries have the capacity to grow quickly thanks to higher marginal returns to investment, which should allow living standards to converge with rich country living standards in the long term (Sachs & Warner, 1995). But the empirical record reveals that poor countries, on balance, have failed to converge with rich ones, leading economists to conclude that convergence is possible only provided certain key economic conditions are met (i.e., *conditional convergence*).[15] Convergence (or the economic dimension of getting to Denmark) is possible conditional on the right policy interventions. In the case of the Northern Triangle, these countries have not converged to Mexican living standards, let alone to those of the United States (see Fig. 2).[16]

[15] For more on conditional convergence, see Fukuda and Toya (1995), Bloom et al. (2002), and Evans and Karras (1996).

[16] The specific conditions that need to be met for convergence are subject to debate. William Easterly notes that the global development community, including the international financial institutions (IFIs) of the World Bank and International Monetary Fund, identified several "panaceas" for economic growth that greatly influenced the economic policies promoted by the IFIs. The initial thrust of these panaceas came from the first wave of Western post-World War II development theorists, including the so-called modernization theorists, who offered a series of economic growth models such as the Harrod-Domar growth model, Walt Whitman Rostow's stages of growth model, and Robert Solow's neoclassical (or Solow) growth model. These models asserted that GDP growth followed mechanically from the accumulation of capital and labor and improving the efficiency of production. Developing countries thus needed to boost domestic savings rates (enhanced by foreign assistance) to achieve target investment levels that would, over time, lead to capital deepening and income growth. Although these models differed in their stylized assumptions (for instance, the neoclassical growth model assumed diminishing returns to capital accumulation, whereas the Harrod-Domar model did not), they nevertheless provided the justification for the IFIs' investment-led growth paradigms (Easterly, 2002,

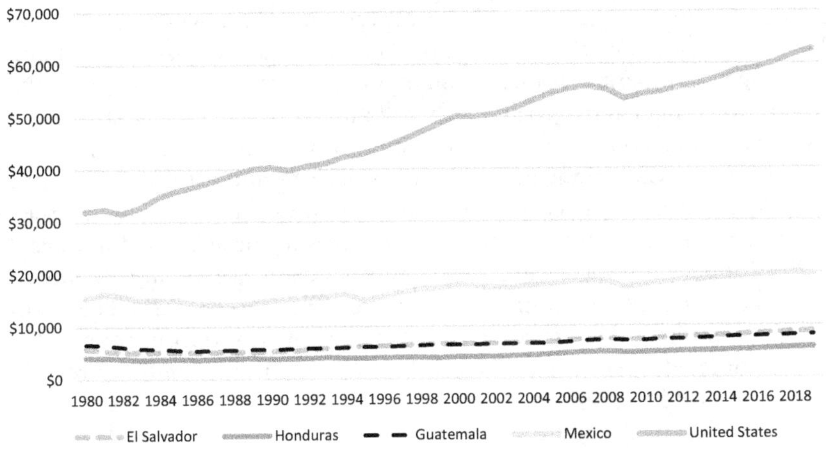

Fig. 2 Lack of convergence: Real GDP per-capita (PPP, 1980–2019) (*Source* International Monetary Fund World Economic Outlook Database and national authorities)

Barbara Geddes further identified that politics can complicate delivering the public goods that are critical for economic development and getting to Denmark. Specifically, Geddes argues that politicians face a dilemma that could undermine economic reform and performance. To

5–70). Other supposed panaceas that proved insufficient to promoting economic growth included, inter alia, higher education spending, family planning, and debt forgiveness. Easterly concludes that development can only occur when a country's institutional matrix promotes the right incentives for governments to support (or at the very least, refrain from impeding) broad-based growth, which itself will be anchored both by capital accumulation and, in later development stages, higher total factor productivity. On the Solow (or neo-classical) growth model, see Solow (1956) and Prescott (1988). For Rostow's stages of growth, see Rostow (1960). For an excellent summary of modernization theory, see Gilman (2003). For a popular Western challenge to modernization theory, see Huntington (1968). These modernization approaches to development contrast with Marxist principles, which argue that the structure of production and global class struggle both within and among states prevent low-income countries from joining the "center" of the world economy from the periphery. They attribute the lack of economic complexity in production and tendency to adverse terms of trade developments that immiserate economic growth (re: the Prebisch-Singer hypothesis, see Prebisch (1950) and Singer (1950). For more on Marxist World Systems approaches, see Wallerstein (1987, 2004). For a foundational approach to Marxist political economy in Latin America, see Cardoso and Faletto (1971).

Geddes, politicians' first goal is to survive in office, which could lead them to pursue short-term electoral benefits (via cronyism and taking advantage of inherent principal-agent information asymmetries) at the expense of longer-term goals (such as building a Weberian bureaucracy and promoting collective action on stubborn development challenges): "...politicians who might otherwise consider offering reforms... will not be able to afford the cost in lost political resources as long as they compete with others able to use such resources in the struggle for votes." Collective action is possible if multiple politicians are willing to forego short-term benefits for long-term gain (Geddes, 1996, 42). The main way to promote reform is to ensure that the gains of reform (popularity and holding elective office) exceed the opportunity costs of foregone patronage (Geddes, 1996, 92–96). The key for development, then, is to create the political conditions with the right inducements and punishments whereby political entrepreneurs and incumbents are rewarded for prioritizing long-term cooperation over short-term patronage.[17] Here, horizontal accountability mechanisms and a strengthened civil society, which can deter and reward cooperation, can help mitigate the effects of the politicians' dilemma.

While there is a debate about *how* countries can get to Denmark, the existence of Denmark and comparably developed polities—including turnarounds such as the rebuilding of Germany and Japan after World War II, South Korea and other NICs, fast growth rates in reform-era China, and recent heady growth in Eastern Europe—indicate that it is possible to get to Denmark with the right interventions. While Latin America lacks obvious success stories of countries that have gotten to Denmark, there have been periods historically when Latin American economies have achieved strong growth spells and where sub-national development outcomes achieve faster per-capita income growth, productivity gains, and development than national averages (e.g., Northern Mexico, which is highly integrated into North American supply chains).[18]

[17] Chapters 2 and 3 provide some examples of inducements and punishments to hedge against short-termism, including using international corruption commissions and by strengthening the role of civil society in the Northern Triangle. In reality, though, there are few easy fixes to short-termism, as politicians will tend to seek to survive as a first-order condition.

[18] On growth spells, see Berg et al. (2012). On the impact of NAFTA on wage growth in Northern Mexico, see Chiquiar (2004). See O'Neil (2015), Kharas and Kohli (2011),

The premise of this book is that Northern Triangle countries can get to Denmark (or achieve lasting economic and political development) with the right set of domestic and institutional factors, including by improving stateness, the rule of law, and accountability. Convergence is possible and should serve as the North Star of Northern Triangle policymaking. But it will be important to recognize that some institutions are more easily transferred than others and to sequence reforms strategically. Per Easterly, there is no "silver bullet" and thus policymakers may be best served taking a portfolio and piecemeal approach to reform. Domestic reformers and their allies should also expect politicians to behave rationally and should thus focus on altering their cost-benefit calculi to promote collective action over graft and patronage to mitigate the politician's dilemma.

2 The Governance Trap

What does the previous discussion tell us about the current conditions in the Northern Triangle and the prospects for reform?

First, Northern Triangle countries have a contested monopoly of force and a mixed ability to deliver political goods to their people. Second, this vacuum of political authority due to the existence of weak states creates space for non-state actors to subvert, co-opt, and evade legitimate political authority. Third, the combination of state strength and scope is broadly misaligned in each Northern Triangle country, insofar as the Northern Triangle states suffer from too much state strength in some areas (e.g., in supporting unproductive public utilities) and too little state strength in others (e.g., the inability to combat money laundering).[19] The Northern Triangle countries also endeavor to do "too much" in some issue areas while failing to do enough in others (i.e., governments strike

and Doner and Schneider (2016) for a good review on Latin America being stuck in the middle-income trap. Doner and Schneider identify that achieving middle-income status tends to fracture the bonds and like-mindedness of coalitions in favor of continued development. As they describe, "big business is split between foreign and domestic firms, labor is divided between formal and informal sectors, and societies overall are riven by high inequality. These cleavages splinter interests and make coalition building more difficult" (p. 611). Thus, a reform agenda should seek to rebuild the political coalition in favor of continued fast growth (what Doner and Schneider call "upgrading coalitions") across these fault lines.

[19] See section on fiscal and financial reforms in Chapter 2.

the wrong balance in state scope). These inefficient state strength–scope combinations are driven partially by the Northern Triangle's weak states—due to contested political authority, it is challenging for the Northern Triangle countries to tailor their state activities appropriately to maximize their positive impact. Fourth, the Northern Triangle's institutions exhibit strongly path-dependent qualities. Since being established, these institutions create conditions for agents to perpetuate them over time. Initial governance weakness thus begets additional governance weakness. Fifth, despite the stationary nature of governance challenges, it remains possible to "get to Denmark" with the right policy interventions. Interventions should focus on helping agents of the state to mitigate the politician's dilemma and remove barriers to convergence. In this way, economic reforms can be seen as an off-ramp to escape the weak governance. In sum, the Northern Triangle countries are stuck in *governance traps*, which is *a path-dependent equilibrium in which weak states with contested authority fail to penetrate civil society and achieve self-sustaining economic growth, resulting in states that under supply political order and economic opportunity*.

A schematic of this book's governance trap framework is presented in Annex 2.

3 Conclusion

Before continuing with this book's suggested economic reforms in Chapter 2, this chapter closes with several caveats of the present study. First, *Escaping the Governance Trap* does not test falsifiable hypotheses nor offer a generalizable theory of governance, economic growth, and migration. Rather, its purpose and methodology are more prosaic and speculative. Its goal is to argue that governance is a key variable in determining economic, political, and social outcomes in the Northern Triangle countries and that economic reforms can enhance governance and thus change those outcomes over time. By elevating economic reforms, this book does not reject the importance of both political and social reforms in the Northern Triangle. Economic reform can and should complement these efforts, and this book aims to fill a key gap in the literature by providing an economic reform agenda for the region. Second, this book relies mainly on analyzing and synthesizing secondary sources to make its case for reform. It does not present a new data set to confront an old problem. Rather, it presents an old problem in a new light, informed by several theoretical and policy-based approaches. Readers interested in first-hand accounts and other primary source data would benefit from perusing the references in each chapter's bibliography and footnotes. Third, this book does not attempt to settle scores and assign blame for how the region got to the present conjuncture. That is not to say history is unimportant, as the region's history is central to this book's governance trap framework that rests on a premise of institutional path dependence. However, assigning responsibility for the region's underdevelopment is not relevant to to the goal of the present study, which is to provide a pragmatic way forward to address the Northern Triangle's governance challenges. This book accepts the fundamental realities facing the Northern Triangle countries and seeks to work within those constraints to achieve lasting change. Fourth, this book at times discusses the Northern Triangle countries as a group, when in reality each country has its own unique history, culture, economic structure, and socio-political contexts. Some grouping is unavoidable, but subsequent chapters endeavor to provide tailored, country-specific reforms. Still, all countries require a path out of the governance trap, and thus some similarities and simplifications are relevant to the present study.

Annex 1: Changing the possibilities of stateness and scope: Potential reform paths

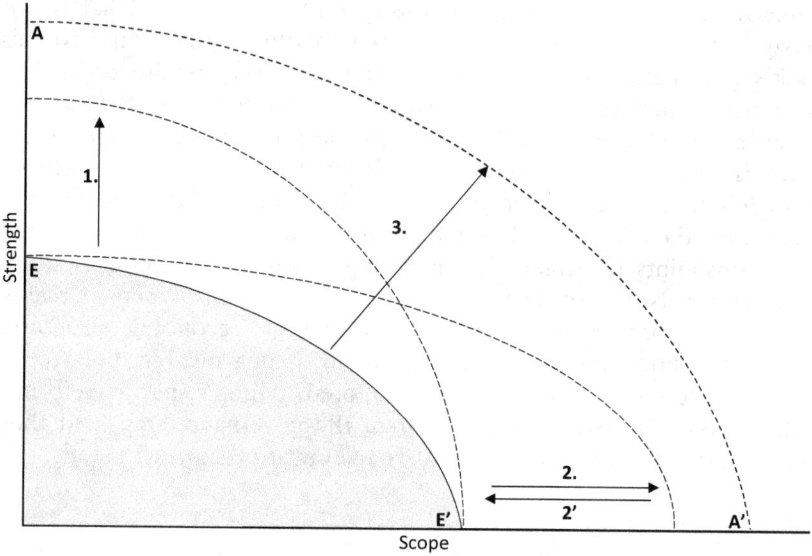

Using Fukuyama's matrix of state scope and strength, it is possible to conceptualize the impact of reform on a state's mix of activities and its coercive ability. Consider a state with an initial endowment of strength–scope possibilities, shown in the figure above as frontier **EE'**. All combinations of scope and strength in the shaded area and along the frontier are possible. A state can choose from a variety of potential reform paths, including increasing its coercive capacity while not changing its scope of activities (reform path **1**) or expanding its scope while not increasing its strength (path **2**), among others. The path chosen should reflect public preferences regarding the ideal role of the state within the broader society and specific activities under question. International partners can provide the technocratic advice and resources to attempt to achieve a desired combination of state strength–scope possibilities. Traditional Washington Consensus-led reform programs, such as those advocated by John Williamson and implemented, to varying degrees of success, in several post-Soviet states, seek to reduce the scope of state activity with less regard to state strength (i.e., a reversal of path **2**, shown above as path **2'**). Such a path runs the risk of abandoning state assets at fire sale prices and creating an oligarchic class of entrepreneurs, which itself poses a risk to medium-term development by, among other factors, sapping the state's strength and capacity and thus reifying governance weakness and underdevelopment. Note that over the longer run, a third path exists in which the polity simultaneously enhances its strength and scope possibilities (path **3**, leading to frontier **AA'**), though practically speaking, increasing possibilities along both axes could be challenging absent significant external and domestic support for reform.

Source Fukuyama (2004a, 2004b) and Author.

Annex 2: The Governance Trap

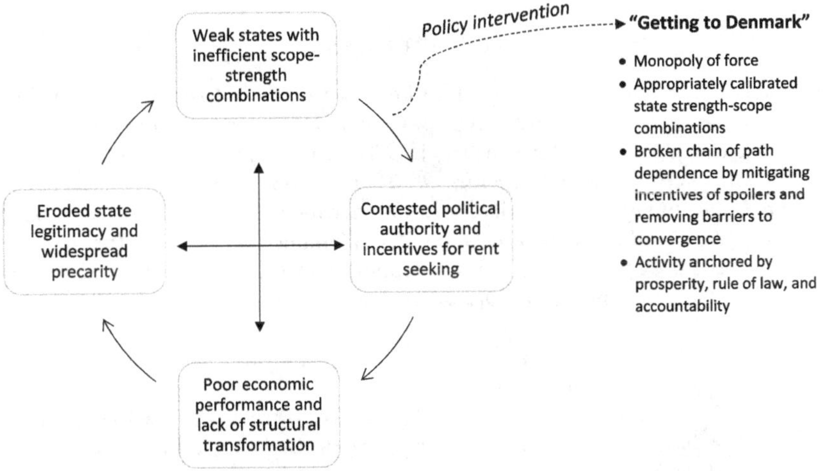

The above schematic is a visual representation of the Governance Trap, which this book defines as *a path-dependent equilibrium in which weak states with contested authority fail to penetrate civil society and achieve self-sustaining economic growth, resulting in states that under supply political order and economic opportunity*. Beginning at the top of the diagram and moving clockwise, weak states have inefficient scope–strength combinations across a range of state activities. This condition leads to vacuums that favor the development of alternative forms of political authority, economic organization, and rent-seeking. In turn, poor economic performance and a lack of structural transformation sow precarity and further erode the legitimacy of the state, and the needs of the population remain unmet. Public trust erodes, and reforms cannot change state scope and strength over time. A lack of legitimacy prevents the strengthening of state capacity, reinforcing governance trap initial conditions. Note that causality in the governance trap is not unidirectional—rather, the governance trap is an emergent phenomenon with many complex causal feedback loops that interact to produce a stable, path-dependent equilibrium. These loops are represented by the crisscrossing arrows at the center of the diagram. Causality could also flow counterclockwise. Policy interventions should seek to break the feedback loops in the governance trap. In so doing, a path of "Getting to Denmark" can be found (represented at the upper-right area of the diagram).

Source Author.

References

Arnson, C. J., & Olson, E. L. (2011). *Organized crime in Central America: The Northern Triangle*. Woodrow Wilson Center Report on the Americas.

Berg, A., Ostry, J. D., & Zettelmeyer, J. (2012). What makes growth sustained? *Journal of Development Economics, 98*(2), 149–166.

Bloom, D., Canning, D., & Sevilla, J. (2002). *Technological diffusion, conditional convergence, and economic growth* (NBER Working Papers 8713) (pp. 1–27).

Bull, B. (2014). Towards a political economy of weak institutions and strong elites in Central America. *European Review of Latin American and Caribbean Studies* (97), 117–128.

Cardoso, F. H., & Faletto, E. (1971). *Dependency and development in Latin America*. University of California Press.

Chamon, M., Hofman, D., Magud, N. E., & Werner, A. (2019). *Foreign exchange intervention in inflation targeters in Latin America*. International Monetary Fund.

Chibber, V. (2003). *Locked in place: State-building and late industrialization in India*. Princeton University Press.

Chiquiar, D. (2004). *Globalization, regional wage differentials and the Stolper-Samuelson theorem: Evidence from Mexico* (Banco de Mexico Working Papers 6) (pp. 1–54).

Collier, P. (2007). *The bottom billion: Why the poorest countries are failing and what can be done about it*. Oxford University Press.

Deudney, D. (2000). Regrounding realism: Anarchy, security, and changing material contexts. *Security Studies, 10*(1), 1–42.

Deudney, D. (2007). *Bounding power: Republican security theory from the polis to the global village*. Princeton University Press.

Doctors Without Borders. (2017, May). *Doctors without borders*. Retrieved May 2020, from Forced to Flee Central America's Northern Triangle: A Neglected Humanitarian Crisis: https://www.doctorswithoutborders.org/sites/default/files/2018-06/msf_forced-to-flee-central-americas-northern-triangle.pdf

Doner, R. F., & Schneider, B. R. (2016). The middle-income trap: More politics than economics. *World Politics, 68*(4), 608–644.

Easterly, W. R. (2002). *The Elusive Quest for growth: Economists' adventures and misadventures in the tropics*. MIT Press.

Evans, P. B. (1989, December). Predatory, developmental, and other apparatuses: A comparative political economy perspective on the third world state. *Sociological Forum, 4*(4), 561–587.

Evans, P. B. (1995). *Embedded autonomy: States and industrial transformation*. Princeton University Press.

Evans, P. B., Rueschemeyer, D., & Skocpol, T. (1985). *Bringing the state back in*. Cambridge University Press.

Evans, P., & Karras, G. (1996, April). Convergence revisted. *Journal of Monetary Economics, 37*(2), 249–265.

Fernández, J., & Tamayo, J. (2019). Industry on the Northern border of Mexico. In S. Weintraub (Ed.), *Industrial strategy and planning in Mexico and the United States* (pp. 197–202). Routledge.

Ferraro, A. E., & Centeno, M. A. (2018). *State and nation making in Latin America and Spain: The rise and fall of the developmental state*. Cambridge University Press.

Fukuda, S.-I., & Toya, H. (1995). Conditional convergence in East Asian countries: The role of exports in economic growth. In A. O. Krueger & T. Ito (Eds.), *Growth theories in light of the East Asian experience* (pp. 247–265). University of Chicago Press.

Fukuyama, F. (2004a). The imperative of state-building. *Journal of Democracy, 15*(2), 17–31.

Fukuyama, F. (2004b). *State-building: Governance and world order in the 21st century*. Cornell University Press.

Fukuyama, F. (2011). *The origins of political order: From prehuman times to the French Revolution*. Farrar, Straus and Giroux.

Fukuyama, F. (2013). What is governance? *Governance: An International Journal of Policy, Administration, and Institutions, 26*(3), 347–368.

Fukuyama, F., & McFaul, M. (2007). Should democracy be promoted or demoted? *The Washington Quarterly, 31*(1), 23–45.

Geddes, B. (1996). *Politician's dilemma: Building state capacity in Latin America*. University of California Press.

Gilman, N. (2003). *Mandarins of the future: Modernization theory in Cold War America*. Johns Hopkins University Press.
Goldfajn, I., Martinez, L., & Valdés, R. O. (2021). Washington consensus in Latin America: From raw model to straw man. *Journal of Economic Perspectives, 35*(3), 109–132.
Goodhart, C., & Radhan, M. (2020). *The great demographic reversal: Ageing societies, waning inequality, and an inflation revival*. Palgrave Macmillan.
Hobbes, T., Guess, R., & Skinner, Q. (1996). *Hobbes: Leviathan, Revised Student Edition*. Cambridge University Press.
Huntington, S. P. (1968). *Political order in changing societies*. Yale University Press.
International Crisis Group. (2017, October 25). *International Crisis Group*. Retrieved May 1, 2020, from Undocumented Migration from the Northern Triangle of Central America: https://www.crisisgroup.org/latin-america-caribbean/central-america/el-salvador/undocumented-migration-northern-triangle-central-america
International Monetary Fund. (2020a). *El Salvador: Staff report—Request for purchase under the Rapid Financing Instrument—Press release; staff report; and statement by the Executive Director for El Salvador*. Internaitonal Monetary Fund.
International Monetary Fund. (2020b). *Global financial stability update: Financial conditions have eased, but insolvencies loom large*. International Monetary Fund.
International Monetary Fund. (2020c). *Regional economic outlook for Western Hemisphere*. International Monetary Fund.
Janetsky, M., & Stunt, V. (2020, April 14). *Migrants take out huge loans to pay coyotes. Coronavirus could cause them to default*. Retrieved May 2, 2020, from Vice News: https://www.vice.com/en_us/article/pke5nb/migrants-take-out-huge-loans-to-pay-coyotes-coronavirus-could-cause-them-to-default
Johns Hopkins University. (2020, September 3). *Johns Hopkins University & Medicine*. Retrieved from Coronavirus Resource Center: https://coronavirus.jhu.edu/map.html
Kharas, H., & Kohli, H. (2011). What is the middle income trap, why do countries fall into it, and how can it be avoided? *Global Journal of Emerging Market Economies, 3*(3), 281–289.
Krueger, A. O. (1974). The political economy of the rent-seeking society. *The American Economic Review, 64*(3), 291–3033.
Krueger, A. O. (2002). *Political economy of policy reform in developing countries*. MIT Press.
Kurtz, M. (2001, Summer). State developmentalism without a developmental state: The public foundations of the "free market mircale" in Chile. *Latin American Politics and Society, 43*(2), 1–25.

Latin America Public Opinion Project. (2021). *AmericasBarometer surveys*. Vanderbilt University.

Latinobarómetro. (2021). Santiago: La Corporación Latinobarómetro.

Leibfried, S., Huber, E., & Lange, M. (2015). *The Oxford handbook of transformations of the state*. Oxford University Press.

Mann, M. (1984). The autonomous power of the state: Its origins, mechanisms and results. *European Journal of Sociology, 25*(2), 185–213.

Marti i Puig, S., & Sanchez-Ancochea, D. (2014). Central America's triple transition and the persistent power of the elite. In D. Sanchez-Ancocha & S. Marti i Puig (Eds.), *Handbook of Central American governance* (pp. 4–22). Routledge.

Meyer, P. J. (2019). *U.S. strategy for engagement in Central America: Policy issues for Congress*. Congressional Research Service.

Meyer, P. J., & Taft-Morales, M. (2019). *Central American migration: Root causes and U.S. Policy*. Congressional Research Service.

Micklethwait, J., & Wooldridge, A. (2014). *The fourth revolution: The global race to reinvent the state*. Penguin Books.

Nachlis, H. (2018). Pockets of weakness in strong institutions: Post-marketing regulation, psychopharmaceutical drugs, and medical autonomy, 1938–1982. *Studies in American Political Development, 32*(2), 257–291.

Nettl, J. (1968). The state as a conceptual variable. *World Politics, 20*(4), 559–592.

North, D. C. (1990). *Institutions, institutional change and economic performance*. Cambridge University Press.

North, D. C. (1991). Institutions. *Journal of Economic Perspectives, 5*(1), 97–112.

O'Neil, S. K. (2015, March 19). *Latin America's middle-income trap*. Retrieved from Council on Foreign Relations: https://www.cfr.org/blog/latin-americas-middle-income-trap

Öniş, Z. (1991, October). Review article: The logic of the developmental state. *Comparative Politics, 24*(1), 109–126.

Plotnikov, D. (2019). *Crime and output: Theory and application to the Northern Triangle of Central* (IMF Working Papers) (pp. 1–21).

Prebisch, R. (1950). *The economic development of Latin America and its principal problems*. United Nations Department of Economic Affairs Economic Commission for Latin America.

Prescott, E. C. (1988, March). Robert M. Solow's neoclassical growth model: An influential contribution to economics. *The Scandinavian Journal of Economics, 90*(1), 7–12.

Pritchett, L., & Woolcock, M. (2002, September). *Solutions when the solution is the problem: Arraying the disarray in development* (Center for Global Development Working Papers) (pp. 1–36).

Quispe-Agnoli, M., & Whisler, E. (2006). Official dollarization and the banking system in Ecuador and El Salvador. *Federal Reserve Bank of Atlanta Economic Review*, 55–71.

Riley, P. (2013). *Will and political legitimacy: A critical exposition of social contract theory in Hobbes, Locke, Rousseau, Kant, and Hegel*. Harvard University Press.

Rostow, W. (1960). *The stages of economic growth: A non-Communist manifesto*. Cambridge University Press.

Rotberg, R. I. (2010). *When states fail: Causes and consequences*. Princeton University Press.

Sachs, J. D., & Warner, A. M. (1995, February). *Economic convergence and economic policies* (National Bureau of Economic Research Working Papers 5039).

Singer, H. W. (1950, May). The distribution of gains between investing and borrowing countries. *The American Economic Review, 40*(2), 473–485.

Solow, R. M. (1956, February). A contribution to the theory of economic growth. *Quarterly Journal of Economics, 70*(1), 65–94.

Swiston, A. (2011). *Official dollarization as a monetary regime: Its effects on El Salvador* (IMF Working Papers) (pp. 1–27).

Tilly, C. (1982, February). *Warmaking and statemaking as organized crime* (Center for Research on Social Organization) (pp. 1–18).

UNHCR. (2015, October 26). *Women on the run: First-hand accounts of refugees fleeing El Salvador, Guatemala, Honduras, and Mexico*. Retrieved May 1, 2020, from UN High Commissioner for Refugees (UNHCR): https://www.unhcr.org/5630f24c6.html

Wade, R. (1990). *Governing the market: Economic theory and the role of government in East Asian industrialization*. Princeton University Press.

Wallerstein, I. (1987). World-systems analysis. In A. Giddens & J. Turner (Eds.), *Social theory today* (pp. 309–324). Stanford University Press.

Wallerstein, I. (2004). *World-systems analysis: An introduction*. Duke University Press.

Weber, M. (1946). Politics as a vocation. In H. Gerth & C. Wright Mills (Eds.), *From Max Weber: Essays in sociology* (pp. 77–128). Oxford University Press.

Woo-Cumings, M. (1999). *The developmental state (Cornell studies in political economy)*. Cornell University Press.

CHAPTER 2

Economic Reform Priorities and the Governance Trap

Abstract This chapter studies the major macroeconomic sectors of the Northern Triangle countries, including fiscal policy, monetary and exchange rate policy, financial sector policy, and structural reforms. It describes briefly how El Salvador, Guatemala, and Honduras have been impacted by the COVID-19 pandemic. It then provides policy recommendations that can help each country create fiscal space for priority spending while enhancing resilience, strengthen their monetary policy frameworks and safeguard external sustainability, improve access to financial services while deterring illicit financial activity, and catalyze structural transformation to improve formalization and competitiveness. Emphasis is placed on inter-sectoral linkages and on the ties between reforms and improved governance. The chapter includes an annex on the impact of Bitcoin adoption in El Salvador, describing Bitcoin and its underlying distributed ledger technology, analyzing the potential drivers of Bitcoin's price changes, and summarizing the relevant decisions and macroeconomic sectoral implications of Bitcoin adoption. Several risks from Bitcoin adoption are highlighted.

Keywords Debt management · Fiscal space · Northern Triangle monetary policy · Northern Triangle financial integrity · Bitcoin in El Salvador

N. Shenai, *Escaping the Governance Trap*,
https://doi.org/10.1007/978-3-030-99023-7_2

The previous chapter presented *Escaping the Governance Trap*'s theoretical framework for understanding governance challenges in the Northern Triangle. It argued that the Northern Triangle countries are caught in the governance trap, which is defined as a ***path-dependent equilibrium in which weak states with contested authority fail to penetrate civil society and achieve self-sustaining economic growth, resulting in states that under supply political order and economic opportunity***. To escape their governance traps, the Northern Triangle countries should pursue reforms to address barriers for improving state capacity, provide critical public goods to their economies, safeguard macroeconomic stability, expand financial access while deterring, identifying, and punishing illicit financial actors, and boost economic growth via structural reforms. This chapter describes these reforms and links them to escaping the governance trap. A summary of this chapter's policy recommendations and links to the governance trap framework is presented in Table 1.

1 Understanding the COVID-19 Context

Before continuing, it is worth considering the novel challenges posed by the COVID-19 pandemic in the Northern Triangle. COVID-19 is a negative global health shock with significant macroeconomic consequences, affecting all the major sectors of the economy. In the Northern Triangle, initial containment measures to reduce disease spread caused a sharp growth slowdown, with contact intensive sectors particularly hard it.[1] Households and firms experienced "sudden stops" to their income streams, exposing vulnerabilities among the most fragile and credit-constrained entities. Everywhere, the pandemic had consequences for the demand and supply sides of the economy, posing difficult tradeoffs of whether to use available policy space to support incomes and undertake other countercyclical measures or to tighten policy to contain inflation, anchor investor confidence, and rebuild policy space. These tradeoffs were especially stark in developing countries such as the Northern Triangle (Gopinath, 2020).

[1] One analysis showed that El Salvador, Guatemala, and Honduras had a higher share of employment in contact-intensive sectors than the emerging market average, while fewer workers were in industries where remote work was possible. See International Monetary Fund (2020).

Table 1 Economic reform priorities and the governance trap

	Crisis	*Recovery*	*The Governance Trap*	*Locus of global support*
Fiscal policy	Support lifelines to offset real economy "sudden stops" caused by the COVID-19 pandemic. Focus on vulnerable households and viable firms. Pending available fiscal space, avoid premature withdrawal of support until the recovery takes firm hold to avoid pro-cyclical policies	Enhance debt sustainability by reducing debt vulnerabilities. Take steps to improve revenue collection and focus expenditures on high-growth multiplier activities. Lengthen maturity profile of sovereign debt stock and explore equity- and insurance-like bond structures, with issuer protections. Focus on fiscal transparency to boost public trust and ensure tax compliance	Fiscal reforms can deter and punish non-state actors that seek to take advantage of loopholes and governance weaknesses to evade tax liabilities. Over time, fiscal reform and additional fiscal space can *increase state strength* and *potential scope of action* while breaking low revenue collection path dependence. Improve incentives for productive investment and boost potential growth	Grants, official sector loans, and credit enhancements (e.g., loan guarantees) to help Northern Triangle countries restore debt sustainability after the crisis. Technical assistance and global coordination to improve tax policy, administration, and compliance, as well as pushing for prudent public investments. Using international enforcement actions to improve public financial integrity and punish graft and corruption via vertical accountability mechanisms

(continued)

Table 1 (continued)

	Crisis	*Recovery*	*The Governance Trap*	*Locus of global support*
Monetary and exchange rate policy	Strong countercyclical monetary policy response via interest rate cuts and easing financial conditions in Guatemala and Honduras. Continued steps to safeguard the dollar peg in El Salvador while managing risks from Bitcoin adoption	Rebuild policy space as crisis abates while enhancing monetary policy transmission. Guard against stagflationary impulse of tighter advanced economy financial conditions. Allow nominal exchange rate adjustment while guarding against second-order inflation effects. Phase out crisis-era unconventional monetary policies to enhance credibility. Manage reputational, prudential, contingent liability, and financial integrity risks associated with Bitcoin in El Salvador	Prudent monetary policy can enhance macroeconomic stability and promote financial market deepening, broadening the supply of loanable funds and facilitating investment and higher potential growth. Phasing out unconventional monetary policies can reestablish monetary policy credibility. In El Salvador, harness positive technological benefits of Bitcoin adoption while managing downside risks. Subject Bitcoin policy to rigorous cost–benefit analyses with a full consideration of alternative solutions, including mobile payments	Technical support to build out local currency yield curves and improve monetary policy transmission. Knowledge exchanges to promote technocratic leadership of independent central banks. Supporting de-dollarization of corporate and financial sectors in Guatemala and Honduras to reduce risks of exchange rate flexibility. Seek ways to streamline global payments, including remittances, in the Northern Triangle countries

	Crisis	*Recovery*	*The Governance Trap*	*Locus of global support*
Financial sector	Avoid credit rationing and guard against financial stability risks caused by real and financial economy sudden stops. Where possible, encourage forbearance by creditors to reduce liquidity risks among solvent but cash-constrained borrowers	Enhance financial system stability by assessing post-COVID financial risks and recapitalization needs. Continue building financial regulatory capacity. Strengthen financial access. Strongly enhance financial deterrence and enforcement capabilities, including through international cooperation	Healthy financial sectors are anchors of broad-based, inclusive growth. Financial inclusion can cut poverty rates, reduce inequality, and raise incomes and growth. Better financial transparency, integrity, and illicit finance enforcement can deny non-state actors' access to the formal financial system, enhancing confidence and safeguarding financial market access	Prioritize international efforts to improve supervision. Increase operational and technical information sharing to address gaps in illicit finance regimes. Encourage engagement via multilateral fora such as the Financial Action Task Force. Harness the benefits of financial technology to improve financial access and transparency. Use international enforcement actions to punish and deter illicit financial activity
Real economy and structural reform	Avoid scarring and hysteresis in output and factor markets via robust countercyclical response to the crisis	Use post-COVID reform period to push for structural reforms	Structural reforms can generate high real per-capita income growth and moving toward convergence. Job-rich growth can incentivize formalization	Technology transfer and economic integration to promote best practices while addressing political economy constraints to structural reform through carrots and sticks. Build regional value chains

Source Author

The Northern Triangle countries responded to the pandemic by loosening fiscal policy to provide lifelines to vulnerable households and firms facing sudden stops to their income and revenues. Slower growth and tax relief measures reduced government revenues. Fiscal deficits widened, leading to an increase in public debt in the context of tighter global financial conditions for developing countries. Debt vulnerabilities rose. The global growth slowdown increased the region's balance of payments needs, creating funding stresses to finance critical imports amid lower tourism, exports, and investment flows. Honduras and Guatemala eased monetary conditions to cushion the real economy hit and preserve the flow of credit in their economy, while El Salvador—a dollarized economy—took other steps to ease financial conditions while undertaking monetary reform by adopting Bitcoin as a legal tender in 2021. All three countries will likely face rising non-performing loans and potentially some financial institution recapitalization costs due to market stress, slower growth, and financial impairment of firms and households. Also, the crisis hit these economies with considerable pre-COVID vulnerabilities associated with high levels of informality, the "digital divide" among high- and low-income households, lingering fiscal risks, governance and corruption challenges (including in public procurement), and a susceptibility to climate change, among others.

While epidemiologists expect COVID to become endemic eventually, with the ultimate timing depending on the availability of vaccines globally, the presence of new and potentially vaccine-resistant variants, and the quality of COVID-19 therapeutic drugs, the crisis will likely leave lasting scars on the Northern Triangle economies.[2] Potential scars include COVID-19 cases and deaths, small business closures and corporate bankruptcies, increases in poverty and joblessness, and the compounded effect of foregone economic activity due to the pandemic. The crisis will likely lead to second- and third-order political consequences in both advanced and developing economies that have not yet been fully felt.

The COVID experience further increases the need for resilience-enhancing reforms in the Northern Triangle countries. It provides an opportunity for the global community to learn lessons from the pandemic and plan for prevention and resilience measures for future crises, including those caused by climate change and extreme weather events, future

[2] For a good summary on how the world can adapt to COVID-19, see Charumilind et al. (2021).

pandemics, and other economic stresses. With this context in mind, the rest of this chapter focuses on how economic reforms can help the Northern Triangle countries hasten their post-COVID economic recoveries while laying the foundation for faster and more inclusive growth.

2 Fiscal Policy

Fiscal policy describes a government's taxation, expenditure, and financing decisions.[3] Fiscal reform is defined as *efforts to strengthen the effectiveness of the public sector's revenue, expenditure, and debt management policies with the goal of enhancing the resilience of public finances and the state's scope to intervene in the economy*.[4] How can fiscal reform help the Northern Triangle countries escape their governance traps? If done correctly, fiscal reform can increase a government's policy options by giving it a larger and steadier pool of revenue. A country with a deeper, broader, and more diversified revenue base is inherently more robust to macroeconomic shocks and has greater policy latitude than one with a narrow tax base. Likewise, fiscal reform may enhance the creditworthiness of a country, making it easier to obtain financing on favorable terms to invest and avoid tradeoffs of sacrificing current income for long-term financing needs. How a country finances itself (i.e., its debt management policy), be it through domestic or external debt, short- or long-term instruments, local or foreign currency borrowing, or variable or fixed interest rates, to name a few modalities, impacts its financing needs and thus its debt sustainability. This debt sustainability, in turn, determines whether a government has adequate room to alter taxation, expenditure, and debt policies without risking debt sustainability and macroeconomic stability. This latitude to undertake discretionary fiscal policy relates to

[3] This section discusses flow variables—such as annual revenues, annual expenditures, and annual deficits—as well as stock variables such as accumulated gross debt. The interaction between these flow and stock variables helps determine a state's fiscal dynamics, including its medium-term debt sustainability and available fiscal space. While both debt sustainability and fiscal space are fraught concepts due to their empirical murkiness, they provide a conceptual guide to thinking about the constraints of fiscal policy.

[4] As argued in Chapter 1, fiscal reform can also create predatory states that sap the economy's productive potential. The challenge for reformers is to enhance simultaneously the capacity of the state to intervene while limiting the scope for over-reaching.

a country's "fiscal space."[5] Increased fiscal space can be used to make priority investments in areas such as social spending, infrastructure, and building countercyclical buffers, in turn enhancing a country's resilience and potential growth. As governments mobilize additional revenue, they have more scope to finance sustainable social transfers, health and education spending, and critical infrastructure. These investments, if executed well, can increase labor productivity and wages, making the country a more attractive investment destination for firms and entrepreneurs.[6]

Fiscal reform can also reduce economic informality, which may in turn improve economic growth. Recent analysis by the International Monetary Fund shows how greater informality reduces government revenues and thus "fiscal space" for priority investments. Higher rates of informality correlate with less productive labor forces and lower incentives to labor force participation (Roldos et al., 2019). Additionally, fiscal reform can improve tax compliance and enforcement, deterring and punishing tax evasion while depriving potential non-state actors of funds to subvert the state, thereby enhancing governance.[7] Fiscal reform may boost an economy's potential growth by increasing total factor productivity and capital accumulation due to targeted investments, such as in roads, railways, and ports. Higher potential growth, in turn, can improve income growth and provide for a more job-rich, technologically intensive and productive, and faster growing economy (Liu & Mao, 2019).[8] Fiscal reform can also improve financial strength and stability, ensuring that a government is itself not a source of credit risk in the financial sector, while ensuring that

[5] For a good primer on "fiscal space," see Heller (2005). For an operational stocktaking of how the International Monetary Fund assesses "fiscal space" in its members, see International Monetary Fund (2018).

[6] Ortiz et al. (2017) and International Monetary Fund (2019b) provide helpful analytical work regarding the importance of social spending to inclusive growth. As the IMF's Executive Board assessed in 2019, "social spending plays an essential role in protecting vulnerable groups, supporting social and political stability, addressing inequalities of both income and opportunity, smoothing consumption over the life cycle, and stabilizing demand in the face of economic shocks."

[7] See Cook (2011) for an excellent summary of how the Revolutionary Armed Forces of Colombia (FARC) rebel group subverted the Colombian government and avoided taxes while levying taxes on coca production, depriving the Colombian government of needed revenue while supplanting features of the Colombian state.

[8] For a good synopsis of practical approaches to estimate potential growth, including accessible lay definitions, see Lipschitz and Schadler (2019, pp. 7–10).

a government has adequate resources to help the financial system should stresses emerge.[9]

2.1 *Fiscal Policy in the Northern Triangle: Prior to and During the COVID-19 Shock*

Prior to the COVID-19 crisis, El Salvador, Guatemala, and Honduras' fiscal prospects were improving, although debt vulnerabilities had increased, especially in El Salvador and Honduras. While debt-to-gross domestic product (GDP) ratios alone do not tell the whole story about debt risks, they provide a topline assessment of how a country's fiscal policy has evolved over time. Since 2008, headline debt has increased in all three countries, with El Salvador's debt increasing nearly forty-two percentage points from 2008 to 2020. While total debt in Guatemala and Honduras remained below regional averages, debt stocks in both countries increased about thirteen and twenty-four percentage points over the same period, respectively (see Fig. 1 and Table 2).

Primary deficits, or the difference between tax revenues and non-interest expenditures, drove the increase in debt in all three countries. The causes of larger primary deficits are explained by country-specific factors. For El Salvador, a rising public sector wage bill and public sector pension obligations, coupled with energy sector subsidies totaling between 1 and 2% of GDP, explain the rise in debt. In Guatemala, the least indebted of the three countries, debt-to-GDP rose modestly from 2011 to 2019, though low overall debt masks fiscal vulnerabilities associated with Guatemala's low revenue base. In Honduras, rising current expenditures on wage bills, as well as transfers to the state-owned power company, known by its Spanish language acronym ENEE, contributed to a widening fiscal gap and additional debt accumulation.

Prior to the outbreak of COVID-19, all three countries took steps to address fiscal vulnerabilities. El Salvador passed a domestically contentious but widely praised pension reform plan that raised payroll contributions, reduced pension fund commissions, capped and taxed some additional benefits, and lengthened the maturity structure of pension bonds, thereby

[9] There is a "sovereign-bank" nexus wherein banks face risks from the sovereign government due to their credit and regulatory exposure while the sovereign also faces recapitalization risks should banks fail. For more on the sovereign-bank nexus, see Feyen and Zuccardi (2019) and Dell'Ariccia et al. (2018).

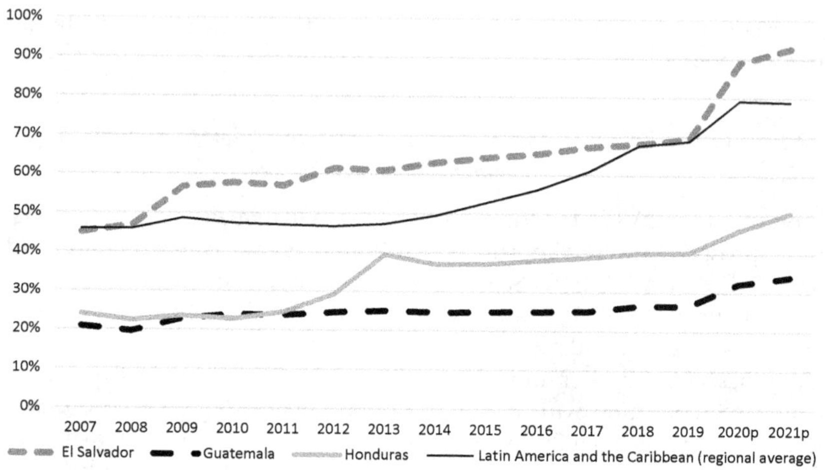

Fig. 1 Northern Triangle debt ratios (*Source* International Monetary Fund World Economic Outlook Database and national authorities)

Table 2 Northern Triangle debt ratios (2008–2020)

	2008	*2018*	*2020 (proj.)*	*Δ 2008–2020 (% points)*
El Salvador	47%	68%	89%	42
Guatemala	20%	26%	32%	13
Honduras	22%	40%	46%	24
Latin America and the Caribbean	46%	68%	79%	33

Source International Monetary Fund

reducing near-term debt service costs and improving its financial position. Anchored by an IMF engagement (specifically an "upper-credit tranche" financing arrangement), Honduras passed a Fiscal Responsibility Law and completed an IMF Fiscal Transparency Evaluation, though ENEE continued to pose a risk to fiscal sustainability. Nevertheless, Honduras was able to access international dollar funding markets and borrow at competitive rates.

Despite signs of positive fiscal momentum going into 2020, the COVID-19 crisis hurt the fiscal outlooks of all three Northern Triangle countries. To contain the health crisis, the authorities adopted several

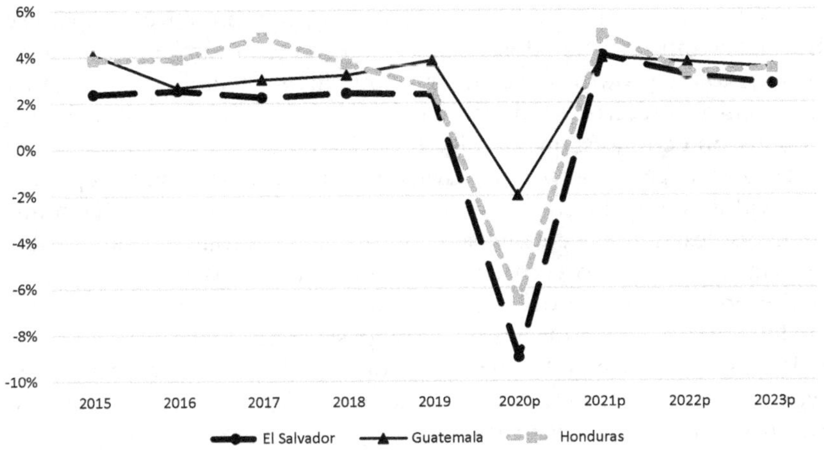

Fig. 2 Northern Triangle growth rates (*Source* International Monetary Fund World Economic Outlook Database and national authorities)

measures, including curfews, limitations on cross-border travel, and social distancing. Contact-intensive sectors were hit disproportionately, while slower global growth further dragged on economic activity. Sectors such as tourism and manufacturing were also disrupted. Together, these forces combined to reduce headline growth in the Northern Triangle countries (see Fig. 2). Slower growth led to declining tax revenues, putting further pressure on fiscal balances.[10] The crisis created demands for fiscal support in the Northern Triangle economies, even when fiscal space was limited. All three countries have adopted measures to mitigate the impact of the pandemic on both public health and on their economies. Emergency spending measures include household transfers, salary subsidies, higher direct government spending on health, and hospital construction, among other support. Declining tax receipts and increased government expenditure have increased gross financing needs. Global financial conditions, while having eased somewhat due to extraordinary central bank actions taken in March and April 2020, deteriorated for the Northern Triangle countries. For instance, El Salvador's bond spreads more than

[10] While growth rebounded in the latter half of 2020 and in 2021, fiscal vulnerabilities remain elevated.

doubled at the height of the crisis, making it prohibitively expensive for the country to tap dollar funding markets. Together, these four forces—slower growth, lower tax receipts, higher spending, and higher risk premia—exacerbated underlying fiscal vulnerabilities and led to a rapid rise in debt, as shown in Fig. 1 and Table 2.[11]

The challenge is now how to navigate the uncertain recovery. A premature withdrawal of fiscal support would exacerbate underlying economic weakness, leading to increased scarring of the real economy and possibly permanent damage to each country's productive capacity. Excess stimulus even after the recovery has taken hold, by contrast, could lead to deteriorating debt dynamics, causing sovereign debt risks to spike and choking off credit to the real economy. Ultimately, post-COVID debt reductions will take time and be a function of both internal and external factors. A faster-than-expected global recovery, anchored by a resumption in travel and tourism, rebound in demand for manufactured goods, higher remittances from the United States, and declining risk premia amid reflating asset prices, would provide an ideal backdrop for each country to address their debt risks. On the other hand, a stalled global recovery amid resurgent COVID cases and vaccine-resistant strains and tighter advanced economy monetary policy, along with geopolitical shocks and higher commodity prices, could require the Northern Triangle countries to address debt risks in a context of declining global growth momentum and tighter financial conditions. In either scenario, additional fiscal reforms should be undertaken to reduce debt vulnerabilities, enhance fiscal resources, and escape the governance trap.

2.2 *Post-COVID Fiscal Priorities*

The aim of fiscal reform is to increase space for priority investments that would boost each country's productive potential, provide social protection for vulnerable groups, and enhance resilience to safeguard fiscal sustainability.

Additional "fiscal space" can come from several sources. On the revenue side, the fiscal authorities can undertake tax base broadening, or expanding the sphere of economic activity that is subject to national taxes,

[11] Slower growth, higher primary deficits, and higher interest rates should increase debt accumulation mechanically. The challenge is reversing these factors in the post-COVID environment, which could improve debt sustainability.

while strengthening tax administration—i.e., making sure the government collects the taxes that it is owed. Together, these activities can increase the resources available to a state. Tax base broadening and raising taxes is not costless, however: in a strict sense of economic efficiency, certain types of taxes create frictions and dead-weight loss, decreasing aggregate welfare. Prohibitively high taxes may, on the margins, decrease the incentives for productive economic activity, which can hinder future growth and thus reduce future tax revenues. Balancing these aims should be the imperative of any fiscal reform agenda in the Northern Triangle. More urgently, the Northern Triangle countries will need to address their chronically high rates of tax evasion, which sap their governments' ability to deliver critical public goods. As Jose Fernández, the former United States Assistant Secretary of State for Economic, Energy, and Business Affairs and Under Secretary of State for Economic Growth, Energy, and the Environment as of January 2022, wrote in 2019:

> Tax evasion is the norm [in the Northern Triangle]: by some estimates, 70 percent of wage earners in Guatemala and one-third in El Salvador do not pay any personal income tax. Economic elites do not contribute their fair share of taxes either, complaining that whatever they pay will end up in the offshore bank accounts of corrupt politicians. (One wonders why the rich even bother cheating. The average effective tax rate for the richest ten percent is a risible 1.8 percent in Guatemala and 4.1 percent in Honduras.) Value-added tax and corporate tax avoidance are also rampant—sometimes high enough to offset GDP growth altogether. (Fernández, 2019)

What are the principles of successful tax reform? One study compared the tax reform experiences of Cambodia, Georgia, Guyana, Liberia, and Ukraine, and found that best practices for successful tax reform include reducing tax exemptions and simplifying the tax code; introducing efficient taxes such as value-added taxes (VATs), which complement indirect taxes such as household and corporate income levies and tend to raise revenue quickly; strengthening tax administration via improved human resources at the tax authorities, better information technology, easier and costless filing; and enhanced audit (Akitoby, 2018). Marcelo Bergman found that successful tax reform efforts require changing the prevailing public perceptions of the legitimacy of tax authorities. Comparing the experiences of Argentina and Chile, Bergman argued that in Argentina social attitudes regarding the legitimacy of the state caused an equilibrium of noncompliance, whereas in Chile, stronger norms and a greater perception of state legitimacy increase the credibility of deterrence via enforcement actions and thus strengthened tax compliance, leading to an equilibrium of compliance (Bergman, 2010). For an additional regional perspective, Aaron Schneider wrote a volume on state-building and tax regimes in Central America, with a focus on the Northern Triangle countries. His work, which is grounded in *fiscal sociology*, argues that cohesion of the state's transnational elites explains the success of state-building in Central America. El Salvador's elites were comparatively more cohesive and dominant than in Guatemala, for instance, which explains why a state-building project took hold in El Salvador but not in Guatemala (Schneider, 2012). These studies indicate that improving tax compliance will require much stronger revenue authorities capable of punishing non-compliant entities, be they households or firms, while deterring future evasion, introducing new taxes, and streamlining administration. As Bergman shows, public perceptions regarding the legitimacy of such actions help explain why some taxation policies are viewed as credible (and thus induce compliance) while others are not (and instead induce free-riding). Drawing on Schneider, building a cohesive base of economic elites that can hold states accountable and push for greater state-building can determine the success of tax reform efforts. The crucial factor, then, is political will for the government to take a larger role in the economy with a clear mandate from the public to do more on taxation (Akitoby, 2018).

Perceptions of the misuse of public funds can reduce the political will and public mandate for the government to "do more" and subsequently hamper revenue mobilization efforts, which is why in addition to tax reform, it will be important for each Northern Triangle country to assess its medium-term fiscal spending dynamics, both within the central government and within contingent entities. Assessing the impact of spending reform would require the national authorities to conduct a dispassionate and apolitical cost–benefit analysis to deprioritize the lowest multiplier spending while maintaining space for priority investments.

One area of focus could be containing the public sector wage bill in all three counties. For example, in El Salvador, public sector wages and salaries accounted for about half of total current expenditures in 2019. Achieving consensus to contain public sector wages is always fraught—typically, bureaucracies are well-represented and core constituents of the governing parties. In the Northern Triangle, some public employees hold their positions due to patronage and not merit. So, ensuring that the tendency toward patronage in the civil service can improve the quality of public services, efficiency of spending, and rationalize the wage bill. Studying the case of civil service reform in Mexico, Mauricio I. Dussauge Laguna argued that while patronage and corruption did adversely impact merit-based personnel policies implementation in Mexico, more specific policy design issues may have also impeded this reform effort. It is thus important to get the institutional design aspect right in tackling the public sector wage bill, which can help overcome more durable social practices such as patronage (Dussauge Laguna, 2011). Another study found that containing the wage bill is often best achieved in the context of broader structural reforms that raise aggregate productivity and thus living standards and incomes. Furthermore, successful measures should be accompanied by strong dialogues between public sector workers and their representatives and the country's fiscal authorities (Forni & Escolano, 2014).

Safeguarding productive public investment should also be a key priority for the Northern Triangle countries. Government investments in public goods such as roads, ports, and power plants could help facilitate the private sector by addressing structural bottlenecks to economic activity. Prudent project selection and technocratic management of projects are essential to ensure that the benefits generated by these investments are worth their cost. Nevertheless, it is hard to disentangle public procurement associated with infrastructure investment from the vast web of governance vulnerabilities and corruption enveloping the Northern Triangle countries. In Honduras, Daniel Sabet finds that corruption covering the embezzlement of social funds, procurement, organized crime, and patronage, is a key input into the political process and can be conceptualized as a political "operating system" for the country. The absence of credible accountability mechanisms (specifically vertical accountability from international corruption commissions and the U.S. courts, for example, and horizontally through the Honduran state, such as Congress and the criminal justice system) allows this system to perpetuate itself over time. While public protests and civil society activism can serve as a check against some of the most egregious cases of corruption, so far public outcry has not been enough to change the current equilibrium of corruption (Sabet, 2020). Here, multilateral lenders, foreign donors, and partners have a critical role to play in encouraging transparent public procurement to enhance the efficiency of investment, including by conditioning assistance on fiscal transparency measures and measures to strengthen public access to beneficial ownership of key assets and companies that receive public procurement access (Purcell & Rossi, 2019). Public–private partnership structures may provide an additional layer of technocratic control over projects, with the recognition that high standards for selecting private partners is critical to success.[12]

Prudent debt management practices can help further mitigate fiscal risks. When possible, each country should look to extend the weighted average maturity of its debt stock, taking advantage of favorable periods of global investor risk tolerance. There exists a tradeoff between borrowing costs and rollover risks: in general, the shortest dated sovereign liabilities have the lowest yield and thus lowest cost, however they need to be refinanced more regularly, thus exposing sovereigns to refinancing risks should creditors refuse to roll over a sovereign's maturing obligations. The spread between short- and long-dated borrowing can compress during periods of heightened investor risk appetite caused by, for instance, accommodative advanced-economy monetary policy or during perceived economic breakthroughs in a prospective borrower During these periods, it may be beneficial for a country to issue longer-dated debt at a slightly higher cost to optimize between managing refinancing risks and reducing overall financing costs. Other measures to reduce debt risks include developing the local currency bond market and when possible, issuing debt in local currency.[13] Doing so would provide a more reliable investor base and hedge against currency-related sovereign debt risks associated with a depreciating currency.

Additionally, each Northern Triangle country should consider newer forms of debt that have embedded issuer protections, such as collective-action clauses (CACs). CACs are embedded options in which a majority of bondholders (often set at a threshold of seventy-five percent or greater) can agree to the terms of a debt restructuring when an issuer faces debt

[12] Frank Beckers and Uwe Stegemann highlight some lessons learned of using public–private partnerships for infrastructure investment, see Beckers and Stegemann (2021).

[13] Hashimoto et al. (2021) provide a good operational summary of steps countries can take in developing their government local currency bond markets, including by building out their local currency bond yield curves. The authors provide a summary of actions taken in Honduras to create an inter-bank market for liquidity, which is a precursor for building out the short end of the yield curve (see pp. 104–105).

distress and impose those terms on all bondholders (even those that may be seeking a "better deal" by holding out or engaging in protracted litigation). While in theory, bonds with CACs should sell at a discount to similar bonds without CACs due to their embedded optionality, several observers have found that CACs do not require significant price concessions on behalf of issuers. While these studies suffer from some selection bias (as most bonds were issued at a time of declining global real interest rates and accommodative advanced economy post-global financial crisis monetary policy), they do offer prima facie evidence that issuer protections may not materially impact the ability of frontier and emerging market borrowers to obtain favorable interest rates (Stolper & Dougherty, 2017).[14] By 2019, all three Northern Triangle countries had issued international sovereign bonds with some form of CACs. Making sure that maturing sovereign debt is reissued with CACs and maintaining this practice should be the norm for all three countries (International Monetary Fund, 2019a).

Going forward, global best practices related to external debt will continue to evolve, and all three Northern Triangle countries may stand to benefit from certain trends and new instruments, such as the development of state-contingent debt instruments (SCDIs) and catastrophe bonds (CAT). SCDIs are bonds that have equity-like features, such as payments linked to the state of certain variables such as GDP and commodity prices. In the Northern Triangle's case, they could explore debt linked to GDP, tourism flows, or remittances flows. While take-up of SCDIs is currently limited, it is possible that a potential wave of post-COVID debt restructurings could renew investor interest in these instruments (Cohen et al., 2020).[15] Moreover, the Northern Triangle's

[14] For some additional background on collective action clauses, including their original motivation in the wake of Argentina's early 2000s default, see Sobel (2016). CACs are useful for potential debt restructurings due to the lack of a global sovereign debt restructuring mechanism (SDRM), which is akin to an international bankruptcy mechanism for countries. For more background on the SDRM, see Krueger (2002) and Krueger and Hagan (2005).

[15] Ángel Ubide and Eduardo Levy Yeyati find that GDP-linked bonds may make sense in theory, but they create incentives for issuing countries to cook their GDP statistics to reduce their debt service burdens. There is also a perverse incentive to reduce growth to reduce debt payments. The authors claim that these temptations were present in Argentina, which issued GDP-linked bonds in the early 2000s Ubide and Levy Yeyati (2015). Still, as argued by Cohen et al., equity-like debt structures have promise for countries that will adhere to their terms in good faith.

geography makes it vulnerable to various catastrophic risks, such as hurricanes and earthquakes. CATs pay out similarly to insurance contracts in which the issuer makes periodic interest payments on the underlying security. If the selected event occurs at a predetermined criterion (e.g., an earthquake of sufficiently large magnitude), then the bond issuer receives a payout from the bondholders. In this way, CAT bonds allow a risk transfer from issuers to bondholders and provide countercyclicality to issuers, as the payouts tend to occur at a time of acute fiscal needs. To date, CAT bonds have been issued by several countries in Central America and the Caribbean to guard against earthquake and tropical cyclone fiscal risk. In the Northern Triangle, there may be advantages to issuing CAT bonds to guard against the increasing risk of climate change (World Bank, 2021).[16] The model previously employed by the World Bank's Capital-at-Risk Notes Program, in which CAT bonds provide insurance to a regional risk-pooling facility to ensure multiple vulnerable countries, may be replicable in the Northern Triangle, provided the countries agree to enter jointly into such an arrangement. Issuing these instruments could help enhance the medium-term fiscal sustainability of all Northern Triangle countries by reducing their vulnerability to disorderly debt restructurings (including holdout creditors), building a debt profile that is more equity-like and thus more robust to volatile macroeconomic conditions, and providing insurance against catastrophic risks, which may be increasing in frequency and magnitude due to climate change, particularly in the case of hurricanes.[17]

2.3 *Fiscal Policy and the Governance Trap*

Fiscal reform can help the Northern Triangle countries escape their governance traps. Recall from Chapter 1 that one of the key features of the governance trap is the under supply of political order. This contested political authority creates space for non-state actors to subvert, co-opt, and evade legitimate political authority. In the case of the Northern

[16] For more on the Caribbean CAT bond program, see World Bank (2014).

[17] For a synopsis of the impact of climate change on the Northern Triangle, including on migration flows, see Seligman (2019).

Triangle, these political vacuums are filled by transnational criminal organizations (TCOs). Contested political authority is both a symptom and a cause of the Northern Triangle's weak states.

There is a nexus between fiscal reform and improved governance, namely that strengthening the state's ability to extract revenues permits it to deliver key goods and services, improves its legitimacy, and strengthens overall macroeconomic resilience and potential growth. Fiscal reform, for instance through improved revenue collection and enforcement of penalties for non-compliance with tax laws, can provide a deterrent for tax evasion. Enhanced fiscal transparency can alter norms regarding tax compliance in the Northern Triangle by increasing confidence in the government's ability to act as a prudent steward of public resources. Rationalized expenditures can reduce wasteful spending, while greater fiscal space can enable prudent investments in social spending and key infrastructure, with positive spillovers to growth. Reduced debt vulnerabilities likewise can have positive externalities to other sectors of the economy as well. In the context of this book's governance trap framework, fiscal reform can help the Northern Triangle countries "get to Denmark" by addressing weak state initial conditions, per Michael Mann and Robert Rotberg (see Chapter 1). Yet the paradox of fiscal reform is that the same agents that are required to shepherd the reform process (i.e., incumbent political actors) are the same parties who benefit from existing weak institutional structures. Thus, to escape the politician's dilemma (per Barbara Geddes), horizontal and vertical accountability mechanisms need to be strengthened, and international partners can help deliver in this area. Sequencing reforms is another key consideration. Should reformers address corruption before attempting to increase public revenues? Is there a risk of cutting public sector wages when growth momentum is slowing, possibly leading to pro-cyclical fiscal austerity? Ultimately, there is no one-size-fits-all approach to these questions of sequencing. Reformers should keep in mind that most fiscal reform creates distributional winners and losers, which can lead to political contestation. There is also a need for reformers to show early results to improve the societal consensus for reform. Therefore, sequencing of reforms should look to spread out the costs of reform over a sufficiently long period while frontloading benefits.

Fiscal policy does not exist in a vacuum, and public finances have significant links to other sectors of the economy. Fiscal policy is linked to real economic activity, impacting both the economy's actual growth (via fiscal multipliers due to fiscal expenditures and revenues) and potential growth (by impacting labor and capital supply and the productivity of these factors of production). Sound fiscal policy can enable the smooth functioning of the real economy, while growing fiscal vulnerabilities and resulting debt crises can immiserate growth. Fiscal policy can also impact monetary and financial policy by carving out space for independent central banks to make decisions related to the money supply and exchange rate based on a technocratic evaluation of economic circumstances, rather than political imperatives. Sound fiscal policy also decreases the impetus toward fiscal dominance, in which unsustainable deficits (with a concomitant lack of market financing) drag the monetary authorities into printing currency and monetizing public debt, jeopardizing inflation targets and setting off price-wage spirals. Likewise, it is often the domestic financial system that is most exposed to the sovereign, such that debt restructurings and write-downs often impair bank health due to realized losses in the banking system. Well-managed fiscal policy can reduce term and risk premia for the entire economy, enhancing banking sector resilience and creating space for financial institutions to originate credit to the private sector. In sum, prudent fiscal policy is a critical ingredient to escaping the governance trap.

3 Monetary and Exchange Rate Policy

Monetary policy describes the decisions made by a country's central bank regarding the management of the domestic money supply, policy interest rate, and by extension its exchange rate regime and exchange rate level. Countries have considerable discretion over the management of monetary policy, including by setting their domestic institutional arrangements, legal requirements, regulations, and policy targets of monetary policy. Monetary policy, in turn, impacts the economy's cyclical position, investment climate, monetary stability, and fiscal space. For instance, a central bank that undertakes significant monetary base expansions (such that overall monetary aggregates rise too) runs the risk of excessive inflation and price level instability, as well as a potential run on the value of its currency as investors demand a higher premium to be repaid in depreciated currency.[18] Such a policy creates problems for firms and

[18] One of the common assumptions underpinning open economy models of macroeconomics is the condition of uncovered interest rate parity (UIRP), which posits that the

households seeking to obtain market-based financing in both foreign and local currency. Unexpected inflation also erodes the value of savings of individual households and could also create problems for the banking sector depending on financial institutions' ability to pass on higher costs of inflation to consumers. On the other hand, an overly restrictive monetary policy could reduce growth by entrenching negative expectations of future growth prospects. Tight monetary policy can raise real debt burdens via disinflation or deflation, with fundamental effects on wealth accumulation due to foregone income compounding (as more current income is required to repay higher real debt service burdens). Expectations of deflation could prove self-reinforcing, dragging on actual and potential output, spending, and employment. Balancing these impulses, including by ensuring that changes in the price level are neither too high nor too low and at an appropriate rate, such that changes in relative prices provide reliable signals to households and firms, is the key challenge of managing monetary policy (Lipschitz & Schadler, 2019, pp. 95–107).

In the Northern Triangle countries, monetary policy featured prominently in their pre-crisis reform efforts and, in the case of all three countries, in their actions during the COVID-19 pandemic.

In the years running up to the crisis, Honduras took steps to strengthen the central bank's monetary policy framework to move toward an explicit inflation targeting regime. As of 2021, Honduras' Congress was considering a central bank law that would give the Central Bank of Honduras additional autonomy to conduct its monetary policy independently from short-term political considerations. The authorities were attempting to move toward a more flexible exchange rate regime as well, with clearer criteria for using foreign exchange to target specific levels of the exchange rate (i.e., foreign exchange intervention). In response to the COVID-19 pandemic, the Central Bank of Honduras cut its main policy rate about 250 basis points while also adopting measures to ease credit conditions facing vulnerable households and firms, including credit moratoria. Going forward, it will be important for Honduras to continue with its legislative push for adopting the new central bank law while phasing out crisis-era accommodation, as there is a risk that continued

expected change in an exchange rate is due to interest rate differentials, which themselves are a function of monetary policy. For more on UIRP (and its limitations), see Chamon et al. (2019, pp. 9–11).

regulatory forbearance delays needed restructurings, while loose monetary policy can de-anchor inflation expectations, particularly as advanced economies reduce crisis-era accommodative monetary policy (International Monetary Fund, 2021b). Such a downside scenario would have knock-on effects on other sectors of Honduras' economy—for instance, de-anchored inflation expectations would likely raise the nominal cost of borrowing for the government and firms, while a failure to address pockets of vulnerability in the financial sector could reduce the willingness of banks to lend to households and firms, dragging on credit supply amid rising impairments in the financial sector.

Since 2005, Guatemala has had an explicit inflation targeting regime, though the COVID-19 crisis presented a unique challenge for Guatemala's monetary policy (De Gregorio, 2019). During the early stages of the crisis, Guatemala's central bank—the Bank of Guatemala—responded to the crisis by easing financial conditions and lowering its main policy interest rate by 100 basis points. Like Honduras's central bank, the Bank of Guatemala exercised regulatory forbearance by easing the conditions by which banks would have to restructure non-performing assets due to the crisis (International Monetary Fund, 2021a). The Bank of Guatemala also chose to monetize part of Guatemala's fiscal deficit amid rising strains on Guatemala's public finances and financing constraints. As a result, Guatemala's M2 money stock increased nearly 20% year-over-year (y/y) in 2020, compared to a pre-crisis average of about 9% y/y. Guatemala's authorities claimed that these actions were warranted as Article 133 of Guatemala's constitution allows for deficit monetization during disasters and other emergencies. It will be critical for Guatemala's monetary authorities to signal that these crisis measures are not a "new normal" of deficit monetization. Such signals may be needed to preserve the credibility of Guatemala's central bank and maintain confidence in the central bank's ability to meet its inflation target.[19] Early signs indicate that Guatemala's commitment to refrain from further debt monetization appear credible, as evidenced by Guatemala's contained dollar borrowing costs and public statements by rating agencies, such as Fitch (Fitch Ratings, 2021). Safeguarding this credibility should be a key element of future reform.

[19] See Adrian et al. (2021) for a summary on asset purchases and direct financing by emerging markets, including guiding principles for policy normalization.

El Salvador dollarized its economy in 2001. Dollarization is the strongest form of a fixed exchange rate regime, since a dollarized country cedes control over the domestic money supply to import monetary policy from a different, anchor currency. In El Salvador, they have imported the United States' monetary policy by adopting the dollar as legal tender. According to John Maynard Keynes, the benefit of a gold (or dollar) standard exchange rate regime is that it helps with "strapping down Ministers of Finance" by removing the option of debt monetization (Keynes, 1931, p. 206; Lipschitz & Schadler, 2019, p. 108). In other words, dollarization helps ensure that monetary policy goals, including stable prices, are not subordinated to fiscal policy goals, namely keeping borrowing costs low. Theoretically, then, dollarized economies should enjoy some benefit of lower borrowing costs, as they have foregone independent monetary policy to remove the currency risk investors must bear from investing in their economies. In El Salvador, Andrew Swiston finds evidence that the removal of currency risk from commercial loans lowered borrowing costs by four to five percentage points, leading to annual interest expense savings of about 0.50 and 0.25% for the private and public sectors, respectively. Critically, these savings were achieved net of foregone seigniorage revenue, or the revenue received from producing domestic monetary claims at a lower price than what is offered by the domestic market (Corden, 2002, pp. 66–68; Swiston, 2011). Dollarization has also helped El Salvador avoid high or even hyperinflation, which has been prevalent historically in Latin America. Despite the potential benefits of dollarization vis-à-vis fiscal discipline, El Salvador remains the most indebted of the three Northern Triangle countries (see previous section), though it is possible that headline debt would have been higher in a counterfactual scenario of not dollarizing. Additionally, dollarization means that the monetary authorities do not have the ability to print domestic liabilities when faced with certain shocks, such as in the case of bank runs. As a result, dollarized regimes may require additional countercyclical buffers given their lack of monetary solvency. Also, under dollarization, more of an onus falls on fiscal and structural, and to a lesser extent, financial policies to ease movements in the business cycle and reduce macroeconomic volatility. Balancing these costs and benefits of dollarization will ultimately depend on country-specific circumstances.

Despite its lack of a national currency, El Salvador's monetary policy recently garnered headlines when President Nayib Bukele announced that El Salvador would adopt the cryptocurrency Bitcoin as legal tender in

2021 (see Annex 2). The move received mixed reviews. On one hand, as a remittance dependent economy, Bitcoin and other frontier financial technologies offer considerable potential benefit to streamlining global payments and reducing costs to El Salvador's diaspora: according to the World Bank, it costs about 3.5% of total transaction cost to send a remittance from the United States to El Salvador under traditional money transfer methods (The World Bank, 2020), see Fig. 3. With total inbound remittances from the United States worth about $6 billion in 2020, worth roughly a quarter of El Salvador's GDP, a drop of average transaction cost from 3 to 0.05%, brought about by the widespread adoption of Bitcoin, would save El Salvador's nationals about $180 million in fees annually (worth about 0.75% of GDP). These savings would be shared by some of the most vulnerable households in El Salvador, where the average remittance-receiving household relies on remittances for about half of their total income. Furthermore, by adopting Bitcoin as legal tender and accumulating about 700 coins as of end-September 2021 (worth about $42 million), El Salvador's authorities have taken a directional view on the future of the dollar–Bitcoin exchange rate, such that a continued appreciation of Bitcoin relative to the dollar generates dollar wealth for El Salvador's authorities. And by distributing $30 worth

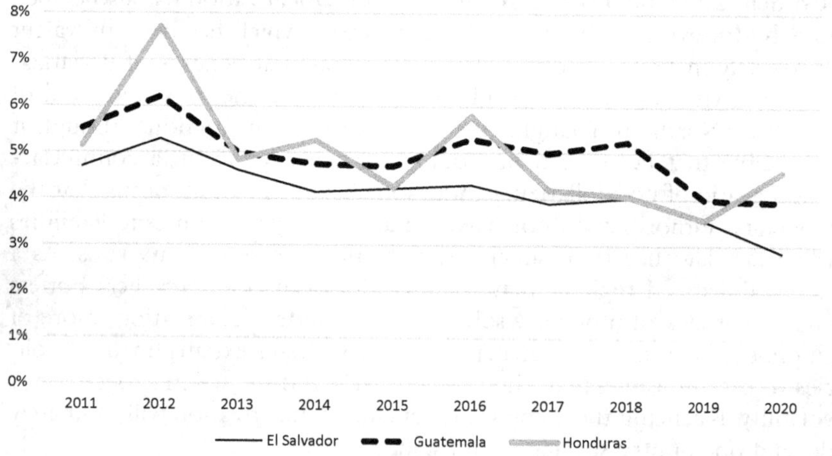

Fig. 3 Average transaction cost of sending remittances to a specific country (percent) (*Source* The World Bank)

of Bitcoin to individuals who sign up for El Salvador's Bitcoin wallet, El Salvador's authorities have made a country-wide and household-level portfolio management decision regarding the country's management of its dollar-based wealth. Should Bitcoin continue to rise in value relative to the dollar, then this speculative purchase will be rewarded, and El Salvador's financial position will improve. If Bitcoin falls in value, then El Salvador will be viewed as having squandered scarce foreign exchange reserves on risky financial speculation (Kurmanaev et al., 2021).

El Salvador's decision to adopt Bitcoin is not riskless. After all, Bitcoin is little more than a decade old, and its future is subject to considerable uncertainty. Some of the risks surrounding Bitcoin and cryptocurrencies fall into three broad areas: prudential risks, integrity risks, and sovereign risks. El Salvador's authorities will need to address these risks as they continue to pursue their Bitcoin adoption strategy.

Prudential risks relate to the fact that the macro- and micro-prudential regulatory regime that governs traditional, fiat currency-based financial institutions and transactions is only partially applied to the broader cryptocurrency architecture today. In many ways, the speed of financial innovation has outpaced financial regulation, and it is likely that international and domestic financial regulation will seek to apply a range of controls to reduce systemic financial risks posed by the cryptocurrency and novel mobile payments systems over time. In El Salvador, it is unclear whether crypto wallets are adequately provisioned with dollar-based liquidity to absorb paper and actual losses in the present value of their cryptoassets, which could trigger capitalization risks. Additionally, there is no Bitcoin-based lender of last resort, which could fuel "run risk" should holders of cryptoassets seek to convert their tokens to dollars *en masse*. While there remain a range of tools to deal with these risks, such as capital charges and funding a lender of last resort with transactions or capital levies, the introduction of these prudential measures could raise costs associated with the digital asset ecosystem and thus reduce some of its appeal on the margins. It is highly likely that the major economies will undertake national and internationally coordinated regulatory drives that could raise costs and reduce the relative attractiveness of cryptoassets

(Muzinich, 2021). The impact of this prudential drive on the returns of holding Bitcoin as a speculative asset remains to be seen.[20]

Integrity risks refer to vulnerabilities related to the fact that virtual currencies may be subject to greater threats associated with money laundering and terrorist financing. According to the Financial Action Task Force (FATF), decentralized systems such as Bitcoin by design lack identification procedures for market participants and facilitate anonymous transactions. Additionally, FATF found that the global reach of Bitcoin implies that certain nodes in the chain of transaction may be in jurisdictions with weak anti-money laundering/combating the financing of terrorism (AML/CFT) controls (Financial Action Task Force, 2014). FATF also argued that virtual-to-virtual layering schemes and other new illicit financing typologies were key vulnerabilities of the virtual asset ecosystem. Balancing the benefits provided by novel financial technologies while safeguarding financial integrity will be critical to the success of El Salvador's forays into Bitcoin (Financial Action Task Force, 2019). Additionally, one study found that virtual assets such as Bitcoin are attractive to criminals for several reasons, including virtual assets' anonymity, virtual (and not physical, or face-to-face) use, decentralization and speed, and variegated AML/CFT landscape, which could make it easier for criminals to use virtual assets to evade existing AML/CFT controls (Schwarz, et al., 2021a). The authors argue that virtual asset service providers such as Bitcoin wallets should take preventive measures to mitigate AML/CFT risk, including applying AML/CFT best practices relevant for other reporting entities such as financial institutions to the virtual asset space (Schwarz, et al., 2021b). El Salvador will need to manage and counteract potential perceptions of a lack of transparency or greater risk of financial integrity vulnerabilities due to its adoption of Bitcoin, which could have negative spillovers for El Salvador's dollar-based market access, including its correspondent banking relationships.[21] For instance, Fitch, a ratings

[20] Taylor et al. provide a helpful summary of different institutional arrangements related to fintech regulation and supervision. As the authors emphasize, domestic and international coordination will be critical to ensure that fintech advances do not pose financial stability risks. See Taylor et al. (2019).

[21] These negative perceptions could be exacerbated by Bukele's decision to dissolve the Organization of American States-backed International Commission against Impunity in El Salvador (CICIES), a vertical accountability mechanism. In this context, Bitcoin adoption could fuel further concerns about governance and corruption vulnerabilities in El Salvador.

agency, noted that Bitcoin could increase AML risks for El Salvador's banks, finding that "correspondent banks could require more detailed due diligence and checks on El Salvador's financial institutions if regulations and controls are not robust enough to avoid tax evasion, money laundering, and terrorist financing" (FitchRatings, 2021).

Sovereign risks relate to the self-limiting nature of virtual assets such as Bitcoin, specifically that as they gain in popularity, including as a hedge against the devaluation of fiat currency, sovereign governments may be tempted to regulate and control the quantity and price of Bitcoin in circulation, thereby limiting its use as an alternative store of value. To understand why governments may pursue this path, consider an argument made by Ray Dalio, the founder of Bridgewater Associates, a hedge fund. According to Dalio, if advanced economies lose control of their fiscal and monetary discipline, then fiat currency-backed safe assets such as U.S. government bonds will likely fall in price relative to non-dollar-based safe assets such as gold and, increasingly, Bitcoin. In these circumstances, there could be a temptation for investors to hold non-U.S. dollar-based assets as a hedge against a monetary debasement (see chapter Annex 2). Dalio cites the U.S. experience during the Great Depression as a precedent. In this episode, the U.S. government, via the 1933 Emergency Banking and 1934 Gold Reserve Acts, seized all monetary gold in the United States and prohibited financial institutions from redeeming fiat currency (dollars) for gold. The 1934 Gold Reserve Act also devalued dollar relative to gold to $35.00 per ounce from $20.67 per ounce as was set in the Gold Act of 1900. These actions were part of President Franklin Roosevelt's broader program to stabilize the U.S. economy during the Great Depression and amounted to a repudiation of the gold standard and devaluation of the U.S. dollar to help reflate the depression-era economy. Applying this experience to the present period, Dalio believes that if political pressures lead to a loose and increasingly pro-cyclical fiscal policy, coupled with ample Federal Reserve money creation, then this dynamic could lead to a run on dollar-based safe assets as investors seek to hedge against weak nominal and negative real returns offered by cash and its equivalents. Recognizing this run risk, and wanting to keep investors locked into the dollar-based financial system, the federal government may seize or limit private holdings of alternative stores of value such as Bitcoin, including by, for example, enacting capital controls to reduce private dollar sales for Bitcoin (DeCambre, 2021; Richardson et al., 2013). The temptation to ban alternative money was not just limited historically to the United States; in 1959, Australia legalized gold seizures, and in 1966, the UK government put capital controls on private citizens' gold holdings (Colvin & Fliers, 2020). More recently, both China and India imposed regulatory crackdowns on cryptocurrency, indicating that this sovereign risk could be a headwind for cryptoasset holders, particularly given the tendency of political economy forces toward greater fiscal and monetary cooperation at the zero-lower bound of interest rates. In El Salvador's case, bans on cryptocurrency could erode the value of its Bitcoin-based savings and increase transaction costs for the U.S.–El Salvador remittances corridor, impacting the welfare of remittances-dependent households and savers that have denominated their savings in Bitcoin.

In the post-pandemic period, both Guatemala and Honduras will need to take steps to rebuild monetary policy space and credibility while addressing potential lingering financial sector weaknesses caused by crisis-era easy monetary policy. Once the post-COVID recovery firmly takes hold, policymakers should prioritize reducing liquidity and tightening financial conditions to avoid overheating their economies. Furthermore, the post-crisis period will provide an opportunity for Guatemala and Honduras to continue to enhance their monetary policy frameworks, including by building out their local currency benchmark yield curves, enhancing inflation expectation surveys to improve their central bank forecasts, and continuing to build expertise within their central banks to strengthen their inflation targeting regimes.[22] Doing so could safeguard monetary and thus macroeconomic stability necessary to induce greater private sector investment in the economy. This carefully calibrated monetary policy could thus lay the groundwork for faster, more inclusive growth in the Northern Triangle, helping all three countries escape their governance traps. Because they have their own national monetary policies, Guatemala and Honduras should stand ready to react to potentially low-for-long advanced economy interest rates while also guarding against a sudden tightening of global financial conditions caused by, for example, a sharp increase in emerging market risk premia or increase in global real neutral interest rates caused by runaway investment demand, a negative shock to the supply of loanable funds, or investor fears of monetary debasement and entrenched expectations of higher

[22] For more on inflation targeting in Latin America, see De Gregorio (2019).

inflation in advanced economies.[23] Given uncertainty to the outlook, these central banks should adopt a data driven and risk-based approach to policymaking, emphasizing the importance of clear communication. Both countries may not have the luxury of looking through potentially transitory inflation. So, they could need to react to incipient inflationary pressures, even if caused by one-off factors.

As a dollarized country experimenting with a dual monetary standard of dollars and Bitcoin, El Salvador has willingly tied its hands and given up monetary autonomy, in effect outsourcing its monetary policy to the United States' central bank, the Federal Reserve, increasingly, to the algorithm underpinning Bitcoin.[24] Therefore, product and factor market flexibility will be the key to promote internal and external balance, given the lack of a nominal foreign exchange rate adjustment mechanism. El Salvador will need to take care that its decision to adopt Bitcoin as legal tender does not fuel reputational risks that could impair the business climate, lead to sovereign bond downgrades, and otherwise challenge the perceived legitimacy of the Bukele government internationally and at home.[25]

4 Financial Policy

The term "financial sector" refers to the institutions that facilitate the provision of capital to entities in need from those entities with surplus capital. Banks tend to be the major financial players in the financial sectors in developing countries, and this is also the case in the Northern Triangle. There are several principles that underpin a well-functioning financial system.

First, banks should *intermediate household and corporate savings to entities in need*. To do so, they emit fully callable liabilities to depositors

[23] Goodhart and Pradhan provide a compelling case for why global real neutral interest rates, after many decades on a downward path, may be set to climb due to changing demographics and consumption habits of capital exporters such as China. Regardless of whether this prognosis comes to pass, it will be important for the three Northern Triangle countries, as small open economies, to be robust to a sudden increase in global inflation and nominal interest rates, which could be set off by a Goodhart–Pradhan style demographic reversal. For more, see Goodhart and Pradhan (2020).

[24] For a good background on El Salvador's monetary history and experience with dollarization, see Swiston (2011).

[25] For more on these risks, see the Annex 2 of this chapter.

("deposits") and make loans to creditors. Balancing the need to provide safety to depositors while taking prudent risks with deposits is a challenge for all financial institutions, including those in advanced economies. Taking too much credit risk could expose banks to losses that could impair their solvency. Taking too little credit risk would imply that Pareto optimal borrowing is not taking place, and that loans that could add to aggregate output are being foregone. Regulators must balance these goals and lean against the excesses of bankers, who are prone to periods of investment manias and despair. Second, banks should have *adequate provisions* in cases of losses. Banks should reserve liquid capital in proportion to the perceived riskiness of borrowers—the riskier the borrower, the more capital banks should reserve in case of loss. Calibrating these "capital charges" is subject to discretion. Here, too, finding the right balance between conservatism (such that banks can absorb potential credit losses without contributing to systemic risk) and risk taking (i.e., "capital charges" that do not dissuade banks making loans) is a key challenge facing bank risk managers and financial regulators. Third, related to adequate buffers, a well-functioning financial system *poses minimal sovereign risk* and, ideally, is a source of sovereign strength. When financial institutions run into trouble, such as due to a loss of depositor confidence amid credit losses, governments often intervene to forestall a chain reaction of bankruptcies from posing a systemic risk to the economy. Thus, there is a public finance and systemic risk management incentive to ensure that banks do not get into trouble by adopting fragile financing structures and speculating on risky assets.[26] Additionally, financial institutions should have the capacity to provide credit to the sovereign during national emergencies, such as during pandemics and natural disasters. In this way, banks can provide a countercyclical buffer to the overall economy, with positive systemic spillovers. The absence of such capacity in Guatemala, for instance, likely contributed to Guatemala's central bank directly financing the government's budget during the 2020 COVID pandemic (see previous section). So, ensuring the financial system has adequate depth during cases of stress is an additional regulatory goal.

One potential risk in emerging market financial systems is foreign exchange risk of the banking sector, particularly in partially dollarized

[26] Governments can mitigate this risk by adopting deposit insurance schemes using paid capital from banks, thereby ensuring that the costs of systemic risk are born by the institutions most likely to pose it.

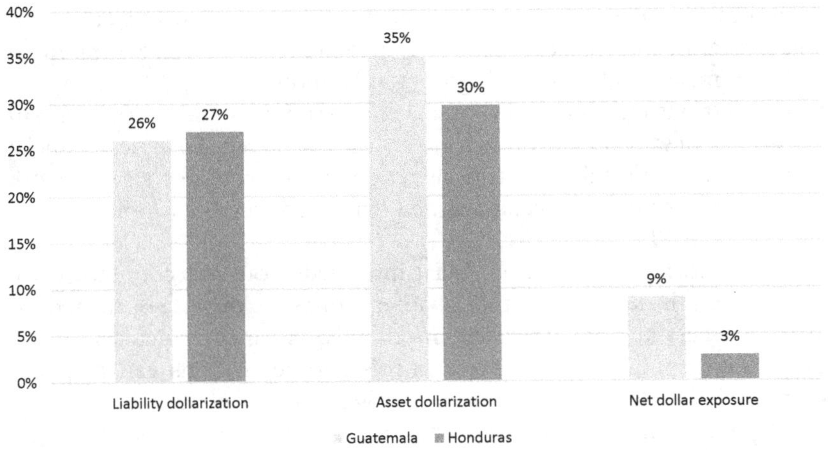

Fig. 4 Dollarization of Guatemala and Honduras' banking systems (2021) (*Source* International Monetary Fund)

economies such as Guatemala and Honduras. In 2021, Guatemala and Honduras had dollar-based liabilities worth about 26 and 27% of total liabilities, compared to asset dollarization of 35 and 30%, respectively (see Fig. 4). As a result, both countries had net dollar exposure of 9 and 3%, respectively, of their banking sectors, implying that foreign currency depreciation would not necessarily impair their financial systems. Rather, depreciation pressures would raise the value of both assets of liabilities, thus providing a natural hedge to the banking systems should the local currency depreciate. Regulators should closely watch the evolution of liability dollarization in their banking sectors, which could pose systemic risks should dollar-based assets decline and net dollar exposure turns negative (i.e., "short" rather than "long" dollars, such that a local currency depreciation reduces the equity in financial institutions). Should liability dollarization increase, regulators should consider a range of macroprudential measures to reduce foreign currency risks in their partially dollarized financial systems.[27]

Fourth, financial systems should provide ***adequate financial access*** to the most vulnerable households and firms. The inability to open a bank

[27] For more on macroprudential tools, see Yilla and Liang (2020).

account can make it difficult for low-income households to save and accumulate wealth, while a lack of credit availability to borrowers with limited assets can make it difficult for high potential individuals and firms to turn their aspirations into reality. Fifth, financial systems should be *transparent* and deny access to nefarious actors. In the Northern Triangle, financial regulation and financial institutions' compliance programs should work together to ensure that revenue earned from illicit activity is not funneled into the formal financial system.

While reforms to ensure financial intermediation and countercyclical bank buffers is important, this chapter hones in on issues related to financial access and transparency. Specifically, enhancing financial access and strengthening illicit finance controls and regulations can help the Northern Triangle countries escape their governance traps.

Why is financial access important to economic development? As the World Bank argues, financial development "promotes economic growth through capital accumulation and technological progress by increasing the savings rate, mobilizing and pooling savings, producing information about investment, facilitating and encouraging the inflows of foreign capital, as well as optimizing the allocation of capital" (World Bank, 2015). Several studies have shown a strong empirical link between economic growth and development and financial development.[28] One of the important benefits of having access to a bank account is the ability for savers to *consumption smooth*—i.e., they can save income for future consumption via the security of a deposit account at a bank. This ability to have a secure form of savings increases resilience among the most vulnerable, who are also most likely to face precarious economic circumstances during periods of national economic stress. Additionally, access to loans allows entrepreneurs with productive ideas to have the resources necessary to pursue them. According to data in the World Bank's Global Financial Inclusion Database, the Northern Triangle countries lag their developing country peers on financial inclusion: about 40% of citizens ages fifteen and older have a bank account compared to 63% of citizens in developing countries on average. The lack of financial access is especially concentrated among vulnerable populations. About 30% of the Northern Triangle's population with a primary education or less has a bank account, compared with 54% in the developing country peer group. The penetration of digital

[28] See Nizam et al. (2020) for a good summary of the literature on the links between financial development and growth.

payments and credit card ownership similarly lag behind in the Northern Triangle. Offered reasons for this lack of financial access include cost, a lack of trust in financial institutions, insufficient documentation, titling challenges that deprive savers of potential collateral, and a lack of funds (see Fig. 5 and Table 3).

One way to improve financial access in the Northern Triangle would be to address bottlenecks to opening a bank account. Some of these obstacles could be overcome with technological solutions, such as improving access to telecommunications and taking advantage of advances in financial technology. As argued by Sahay et al., financial technology has the potential to drive down the cost of financial services, thus improving financial access. The authors also find that digital financial inclusion faces several barriers, including gaps in telecommunications infrastructure and access, cultural norms and other non-economic conventions that raise the costs of switching to new technologies, and challenges with digital and financial literacy (Sahay et al., 2020). Thus, a sustained reform effort in the Northern Triangle should focus on closing these gaps over time, including through investments in telecommunications infrastructure such as broadband internet access and a public awareness drive to boost knowledge of and confidence in financial technology.

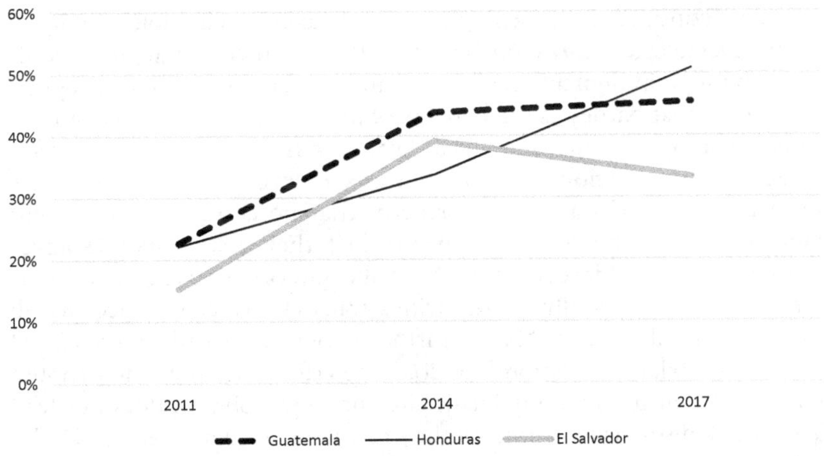

Fig. 5 Percentage of adults with bank accounts (percent ages 25+) (*Source* The World Bank)

Table 3 Selected financial inclusion statistics (percent of population age 15+)[a]

Financial access	*SLV*	*GTM*	*HND*	*Averages* *NT*	*Averages* *LAC*	*Averages* *DCs*
Has an account	30%	44%	45%	40%	55%	63%
Has an account, primary education or less	20%	33%	37%	30%	44%	54%
Made digital payments in the past year	18%	27%	30%	25%	46%	36%
Credit card ownership	6%	7%	5%	6%	19%	10%

Reasons for lack of financial access[b]	*SLV*	*GTM*	*HND*	*Averages* *NT*	*Averages* *DCs*
Too expensive	34%	34%	38%	36%	12%
Lack of trust in financial institutions	22%	23%	19%	22%	7%
Lack of documentation	18%	22%	23%	21%	9%
Lack of funds	40%	43%	46%	43%	28%

[a]Note that SLV = El Salvador; GTM = Guatemala; HND = Honduras; NT = Norther Triangle; LAC = Latin America and the Caribbean; DCs = Developing Countries
[b]Regional averages for Latin America and the Caribbean not available for lack of financial access data
Source World Bank (Values taken from Demirgüç-Kunt, Asli, Leora Klapper, Dorothe Singer, Saniya Ansar, and Jake Hess [2018]. *The Global Findex Database 2017: Measuring Financial Inclusion and the Fintech Revolution*)

Incentivizing credit deepening through financial technology will likely require a concerted effort on behalf of the Northern Triangle governments to invest in digital infrastructure and a financial technology regulatory regime that harnesses the benefits of financial technology, safeguards against macroprudential and illicit finance risks, and provides privacy protections in a region that underinvests in cybersecurity historically. Given their lack of scale, the Northern Triangle countries may benefit from a financial technology dialogue in which they seek to pool resources across countries to address jointly the challenges of financial access. Information sharing, especially on suspicious transactions, can reduce overall risks to financial integrity. Here, further cooperation with international partners and bilateral relationships could be crucial. Each country should take steps to ensure that any financial technology solution does not lead to financial disintermediation of the traditional banking sector. Under such a circumstance, savers may seek to withdraw deposits from banks to move their funds to non-bank or new bank financial technology-enabled firms. These withdrawn deposits could pose a financial stability risk as savers withdraw deposits from banks and banks are forced to seek other, potentially more costly forms of funding.

In addition to improving financial access, it will be important for each Northern Triangle country to improve their financial integrity. Financial integrity refers to the ability of the financial system to deter illicit actors from transferring the proceeds of their illicit activities, such as drug and human trafficking, racketeering, and corruption, to the financial system in order to obscure the illicit origins of the funds—i.e., what is broadly defined as anti-money laundering (AML). Financial integrity also encompasses the steps a polity can take to deter predicate crimes and to promote good governance practices. Together with combatting the financing of terrorism (CFT), AML/CFT efforts describe the behavior of public and private actors to deter and punish money laundering within a given jurisdiction.

Why is maintaining financial integrity important? In short, financial integrity helps protect both economic and political security by denying illicit actors fungibility of their proceeds from illicit activities. Making it difficult for drug traffickers to obscure the illicit sources of their funds can reduce the attractiveness of drug trafficking, potentially diminishing its incidence or at least reducing its profitability. The absence of financial integrity often coincides with weak states with contested political authority. It also threatens the rule of law and political order by furnishing vast resources to criminal enterprises that fuel corruption and violence. Countries with financial integrity risks also may find it more difficult to attract international capital or maintain correspondent banking relationships with other countries. Being perceived as a high-risk financial jurisdiction thus can have macroeconomic consequences. Therefore, the governments of the Northern Triangle countries have an interest in maintaining the financial integrity of their countries (International Monetary Fund, 2017).

While financial institutions are often on the front lines of AML risks, given their exposure to private actors who may seek to mask the illicit source of their funds, governments bear the ultimate risk of AML vulnerabilities. Financial integrity risks can jeopardize a country's access to external financing, threaten financial stability, and undermine trust in a country's financial system. As outlined in Annex 1, a successful AML/CFT regime requires close cooperation between financial institutions, financial regulators (including Financial Intelligence Units, or

FIUs), AML enforcement authorities, political authorities, and international public and private partners. The riskiness of a financial jurisdiction relates to its vulnerability to ML/CF and its related underlying crimes, "predicate crimes," or the actions that generate illicit funds that agents then seek to launder through the licit financial system to mask the funds' ultimate origins, as well as its financial system's capacity to track funds, monitor risks, share information between private and public entities, have appropriate laws and regulations in place, and identify and punish agents that break the system's laws.

All three Northern Triangle countries are exposed to money laundering risks due to their proximity to major drug-producing countries and central location along drug trafficking corridors. According to the U.S. Department of State, each Northern Triangle country has significant AML vulnerabilities. El Salvador's dollarized economy makes it a relatively attractive destination for illicit financial flows.[29] Its capacity and operational AML challenges recently led to it being censured by the Egmont Group, a platform by which many of the world's FIUs exchange data. In 2018, the Egmont Group suspended El Salvador due to "continuous lack of compliance with Egmont Group principles relating to operational independence and autonomy" (Egmont Group, 2018). This suspension prohibited El Salvador's FIU from sending and receiving data through the Egmont Group platform with other FIUs and participating in Egmont Group-sponsored trainings. El Salvador's FIU rejoined the Egmont Group in 2019, though it continues to be hampered by thin staffing and negative perceptions about its lack of operational autonomy. El Salvador also struggles with regulating designated non-financial businesses and professions (DNFBPs), which include entities such as casinos, lawyers, real estate agents, and trust companies (among others).[30] Despite these challenges, El Salvador's Attorney General's specialized Group Against Impunity continues to try AML cases, including against former political leaders and individuals with ties to drug trafficking organizations, including the MS-13 gang.

Similarly, Honduras is vulnerable to money laundering risks due to narcotics trafficking, TCOs, and public corruption such as in cases

[29] The introduction of Bitcoin may exacerbate these vulnerabilities, particularly given Bitcoin's anonymity. See Schwarz et al. (2021a, 2021b).

[30] For more on DNFBPs, see Omar and Hajudin (2015).

of high-level fraud, bribery, and similar offenses. Like El Salvador, Honduras needs to enhance DNFPB laws and regulations. Changes in the penal code in 2020 watered down some key provisions related to beneficial ownership and information sharing related to AML predicate offenses. Capacity among financial regulators is low, and the country is struggling with improving information systems and harmonizing information sharing across bureaucracies and with the private sector on AML cases. Guatemala has similar vulnerabilities as El Salvador and Honduras. Guatemala's congress has stymied efforts on behalf of the Bank Superintendent's office to improve AML supervision and enforcement. Additionally, there are no laws in Guatemala that explicitly prohibit structuring deposits (or breaking them into several transactions to avoid reporting requirements), leading to potential abuse of the formal financial system (United States Department of State, 2021). Third party indicators, such as the Basel AML Index, found that the Northern Triangle's risk scores are roughly in line with the average index level compared to a sample of 110 financial jurisdictions. These results would indicate that the Northern Triangle countries have vulnerabilities, but also some advantages in fighting money laundering, such as the possibility of close collaboration with the United States, a relative lack of terrorist financing risk, and mature banking systems (see Table 4).

To enhance the effectiveness of each country's AML/CFT regimes and financial integrity, reforms should focus on several areas:

First, it will be important to strengthen capacity and address illicit finance vulnerabilities along the entire AML/CFT value chain. Illicit actors will test multiple nodes in the AML/CFT system seeking an advantage. For instance, a low capacity or politically compromised enforcement

Table 4 Money laundering and terrorist financing risk (2015–2021)[a]

	2015	*2016*	*2017*	*2018*	*2019*	*2020*	*2021*	*Average*
El Salvador	4.79	4.69	5.48	5.43	5.46	4.87	4.83	**5.08**
Guatemala	5.78	5.97	6.17	4.95	4.75	5.1	5.12	**5.41**
Honduras	6.27	6.04	5.97	5.85	5.76	5.54	5.52	**5.85**

[a]Scores range from 1 to 10, with higher values indicating a higher risk of ML/TF. The sample average of all 110 countries included in the Basel AML index has a value of about 5.30 and a standard deviation of about 1.20

Source Basel AML Index

authority may be particularly vulnerable to manipulation by private actors. Further, no amount of enforcement and transaction monitoring can compensate for banks failing to conduct appropriate customer due diligence measures (also known as "Know Your Customer" measures); indeed, the chain of AML prevention is only as strong as its weakest link. So, reform efforts should take a system-wide approach and seek to enhance the effective implementation of preventive measures (including customer due diligence obligations) by financial institutions and DNFBPs, promote information sharing among financial institutions and FIUs, including to ensure financial institutions are submitting quality suspicious transaction reports, strengthen the operational independence and reach of enforcement authorities, and deepen ties with international partners such as the Egmont Group, FATF and FATF-style regional bodies (e.g., the Caribbean Financial Action Task Force (CFATF) and Financial Action Task Force of Latin America (GAFILAT)), and the international financial institutions, among other key multilateral and bilateral institutions. Recent steps by Honduras to prepare legislation related to a beneficial ownership registry, for instance, and by Guatemala to prepare an updated AML/CFT law show that progress on these issues is possible.

Second, operational independence is critical to ensuring high standards of financial integrity, especially in countries with large governance and corruption-related vulnerabilities. This need for operational independence stemming from delegated authority, however, presents a paradox for policymakers: how should potentially corrupt actors be induced to delegate authority to agencies with anti-corruption mandates? This is a challenging problem for reformers and, given the intractability of vested interests, could be a place where likeminded foreign partners can help. All three Northern Triangle countries have experience with international–national hybrid missions against corruption and impunity, such as the International Commission against Corruption and Impunity in El Salvador (CICIES), International Commission Against Impunity in Guatemala (CICIG), and Mission in Support of the Fight against Corruption and Impunity in Honduras (MACCIH). Although the results from these hybrid missions were mixed, they do show that hybrid missions with vertical accountability mechanisms, when accompanied by sufficient political will and commitment, can serve as a force multiplier of domestic anti-corruption efforts.[31]

Third, the Northern Triangle countries should develop a culture of domestic and international information sharing to develop a holistic picture of their shared financial vulnerabilities. Indeed, the threats these countries face are transnational and thus warrant a transnational approach. The main barriers to information sharing both domestically and internationally relate to a lack of trust among financial institutions and regulators: banks are reluctant to share privileged information with rivals unless a trusted third party (e.g., an FIU) is willing to guarantee privacy and anonymity of counterparties. Similarly, financial institutions and enforcement authorities may be reluctant to collaborate due to bureaucratic rivalries. These problems are compounded when regulators try to cooperate across borders, where bureaucratic and jurisdictional questions often hamper cooperation. Despite these challenges, stronger collaboration and information sharing among the Northern Triangle countries and with sources and destinations along trafficking routes—from South America to the United States—could yield dividends by reducing information asymmetries and reducing regulatory arbitrage opportunities for illicit actors.

Fourth, much like in the case of improving financial access, financial technology can enhance the effectiveness of the Northern Triangle's financial regulatory and AML/CFT regimes. Novel software solutions, such as blockchain-based payments solutions and centralized data utilities, can make it easier for financial institutions to share information with each other. E-records and digital financial footprints can reduce bureaucratic costs of tracking transactions and cases, thus making it easier for customers, financial institutions, and regulators to transfer data among jurisdictions. AML/CFT controls will likely increasingly harness frontier technologies such as artificial intelligence and machine learning, which can help identify anomalies in financial transactions while lowering the cost of AML/CFT regulatory solutions. The potential advent of central

[31] For a fruitful and balanced assessment of CICIES, CICIG, and MACCIH, see Call (2020a). As Charles Call notes, in both Guatemala and Honduras, Presidents Jimmy Morales and President Juan Orlando Hernández ultimately undermined and rejected CICIG and MACCIH, respectively, once these commissions threatened their political standing and livelihoods. For more, see Call (2020b, 2020c). For more on how international partners can engage these international missions, see Chapter 3.

bank digital currency (CBDC) can also make it easier for financial regulators to track payments, while also reducing the relative appeal (and related anonymity) of cash. Balancing these goals—including financial access, financial integrity, security, and privacy—will require a sustained dialogue among multiple stakeholders. But if implemented successfully, technology could play an increasing role in strengthening the Northern Triangle's AML/CFT regimes.

Financial integrity is linked to governance. Financial systems vulnerable to money laundering are more likely to attract corrupt actors. These vulnerabilities act like a tax on the entirety of the financial system. Governments are denied revenue from the proceeds of corruption; households often lack financial access due to heightened risk aversion of financial institutions; smaller or upstart firms may find it harder to access credit because established players have co-opted existing institutions and enacted regulatory barriers to entry; and the fundamental stateness of the polity, in the Weberian sense, is threatened by the generation and laundering of illicit proceeds. Worse, the existence of these rents perpetuates the incentives for corruption and illicit finance over time, fueling governance vulnerabilities in a path-dependent manner. The lack of financial integrity is central to the governance trap, and tackling these vulnerabilities are crucial to escaping it.

5 Structural Reforms

Structural reforms refer to actions taken to improve the productivity of the factors of production in a given country to boost output and efficiency. If implemented correctly, structural reforms can unlock an economy's growth potential and enhance its macroeconomic resilience. Structural reforms refer to policy interventions aimed at the supply side of the economy. Supply can come from three sources: labor, capital, and technology. Structural reforms target improving an economy's total factor productivity, which Leslie Lipschitz and Susan Schadler describe as the "institutional and technological characteristics of the economy that determine how efficiently labor and capital can be combined to produce output." Countries with higher total factor productivity growth grow at a faster rate than countries with lower factor productivity growth when controlling for capital accumulation and labor supply growth (Lipschitz & Schadler, 2019, pp. 25, 9–11). In turn, stronger growth, underpinned by a vibrant private sector and rising worker productivity, has direct links to governance: higher growth can enhance debt sustainability, raise wages and capital rents, and lead to a virtuous cycle of non-inflationary growth. Rising wages can attract workers into the formal sector, reducing the relative appeal of informal or illicit activities, further channeling rents into the formal economy and leading to higher revenue mobilization. Stronger wage and job growth can reduce the incentives to emigrate, since rising wages in developing countries can reduce the wage differential between countries (Savoy & Sady-Kennedy, 2021).

There are many types of structural reforms. Drawing on World Bank data, Lipschitz and Schadler identify five key components of total factor productivity, which in turn suggest potential areas for reform. These components are: technology (enabled by technological transfers such as through foreign direct investment), infrastructure (which can drive down the cost of production and enhance economic efficiency), human capital (i.e., years of educational attainment and technical skills earned through on-the-job training, apprenticeships, and formal and informal schooling), the business environment and governance (reducing obstacles to productive exchange), and political and economic stability (Lipschitz & Schadler, 2019, pp. 25–26). The World Economic Forum compiles a multifaceted assessment of global competitiveness that draws on several sources and provides a numeric score between 1 and 7 on several competitiveness rankings. The Northern Triangle countries on average tend to underperform Mexico and the United States in terms of property rights, the quality of infrastructure, FDI and technology transfer, business costs of crime and violence, and health and primary education. However, aside from the business costs of crime and violence, the Northern Triangle countries score roughly in line with regional averages for Latin America and the Caribbean (see Fig. 6). These data suggest that reform efforts to improve infrastructure and reduce crime and violence could yield benefits to each country's competitiveness. Indeed, one study found that in a sample of Latin American countries, improving infrastructure quality to the median of sample countries could increase long-term potential GDP growth by ten basis points. Over a long period with compounding, minor changes in

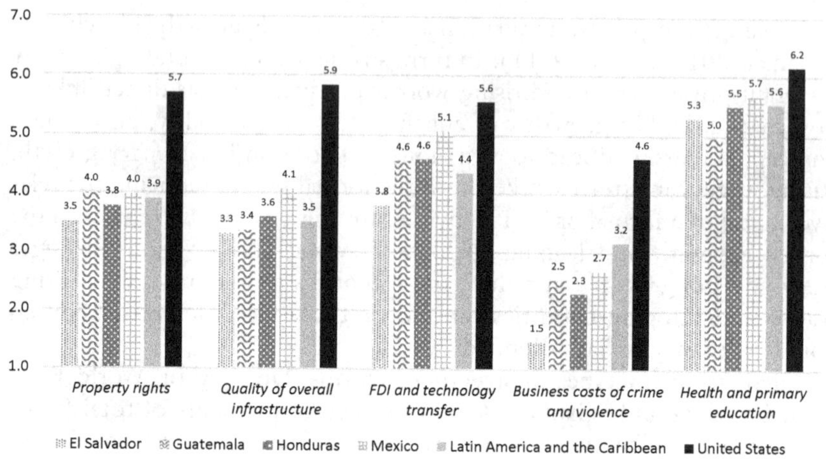

Fig. 6 Global competitiveness index (2017–2018) (*Source* World Economic Forum)

growth rates can have large effects on total income decades later (Lanau & Roldos, 2017). In the Northern Triangle, poor infrastructure hurts firms that want to take advantage of greater economic integration across the Northern Triangle countries or exporters that want to get their products to the global market at a low cost.

This book does not provide a granular assessment of the types of structural reforms the Northern Triangle countries should undertake. Rather, it will be up to the Northern Triangle countries themselves to identify reform gaps and to prioritize specific structural reforms to fill these gaps over time. Certainly, international partners have a role to play, but the most successful reform efforts have a strong sense of national ownership, for which no amount of policy advice and foreign money can substitute. Nevertheless, it is possible to offer a few lessons for potential reformers when thinking about structural reforms.

First, it may be advisable to push for structural reforms when it appears as though they are the least needed. In other words, reformers should consider undertaking structural reforms when the economy is growing at its potential. Often, structural reform agendas are pushed by external actors during periods of macroeconomic distress. But during cyclical downswings, leaders are often consumed by stemming the tide of crisis. Achieving domestic consensus can be challenging. The difficultly for policymakers, then, is to make the case for structural reforms when conditions are stable—i.e., precisely at the point when publicly they may seem the least needed.[32] Second, structural reformers should guard against adopting overly anti-statist policies. During the heyday of the Washington Consensus in the 1990s, the international financial institutions pushed for privatizations and a devolution of state activity to the private sector. Such a culling of state scope runs the risk of entrenching a narrow band of economic elites that are able to purchase government assets at depressed values, as occurred in several post-Soviet states.[33] Third, sequencing matters. Pushing for financial sector reforms and financial technology prior to upgrading broadband and telecommunications networks, for instance, may hamper the effectiveness of financial inclusion efforts. Reformers should thus move in stages. Fourth, scale can be a durable competitive advantage. As evidenced by the American and European experiences, economic integration can help individual countries gain bargaining power and strong internal markets in the face of global competition. As small open economies, the Northern Triangle countries could benefit from working more closely together on addressing shared barriers to inclusive growth, such as harmonizing regulatory practices, building communications, transportation, and energy interconnections, and reducing trade protectionism. Fifth, reformers should recognize that most major regulatory pushes invite counterreactions, and thus continued vigilance against backsliding and early efforts to lock-in reforming gains

[32] Kurt Weyland argues that crises provide opportunities for leaders to push for bold reforms in Argentina, Brazil, Peru, and Venezuela. Building on insights from behavioral economics and behavioral finance, Weyland takes a prospect theory-backed approach to analyzing reform efforts in these four countries. He finds that challenging domestic conditions create the conditions by which reluctant populaces may back far-reaching (or "draconian") reforms. While crises can be useful critical junctures in which political and economic entrepreneurs can push for key reforms, undertaking macroeconomic or structural adjustment in a non-crisis period may prove more durable, as evidenced by the mixed legacies of the reform efforts studied by Weyland. See Weyland (2004).

[33] One example of such excessive downsizing of state scope occurred in the 1990s Argentina, in which Argentine President Carlos Menem pushed for privatizations of state-owned enterprises in industries such as in communications and energy. Despite some initial success, during Argentina's early 2000s economic crisis, many of these privatized enterprises were re-nationalized. See Baer and Montes-Rojas (2010).

are key. Even if the polity as a whole may benefit from reforms, most reform efforts can undermine vested interests that can spoil even the most determined reformer. Building a political coalition in favor of reform may require providing some concessions to incumbent interests. While these concessions can reduce the depth of reforms, they could safeguard against backsliding.

6 Conclusion

This chapter took a sectoral approach to economic reforms in the Northern Triangle. It focused on fiscal policy, monetary and exchange rate policy, financial sector policy, and structural reforms, and explained how reforms in these areas can help the Northern Triangle countries enhance their governance and escape the governance trap. These reforms are not silver bullets. Their relationship to improved governance does not conform to traditional cause–effect relationships, particularly because many reform dynamics have positive and negative feedback loops. Even if causal links are confounding, this chapter still presented evidence and logic that explained why creating fiscal space and reducing fiscal vulnerabilities, safeguarding monetary and exchange rate stability, enhancing financial access and deterring illicit financial activity, and pushing for improvements in potential growth via structural reforms, can help the Northern Triangle countries escape their governance traps. But as this chapter makes clear, the scope of work ahead is considerable, and the domestic will and ability to reform can be limited. It is here where international partners can help the Northern Triangle countries, providing timely support to help them push for economic reform efforts. The role of international partners is examined in chapter three.

Annex 1: Schematic Of Financial Integrity

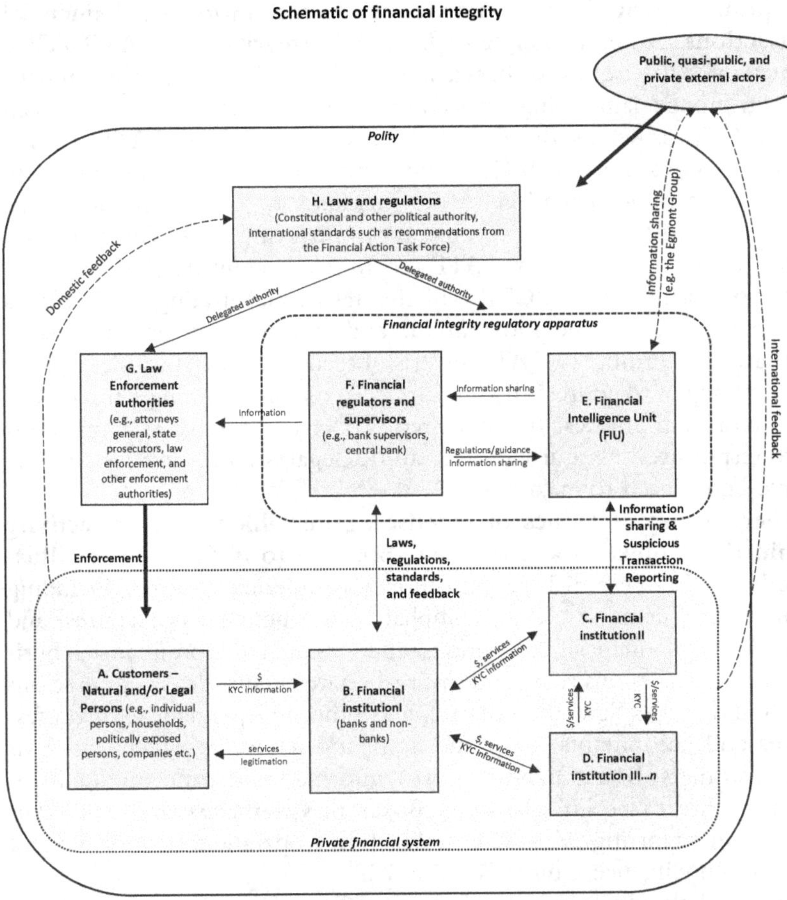

The above diagram shows the different steps of maintaining a transparent financial system with high standards of financial integrity. The boxes within the polity (Boxes A through H) represent major actors within a polity's financial system. The outermost box demarks the polity, with the upper-right oval representing the influence of public, quasi-public, and private external actors on all three levels of the schematic.

Note that this diagram is illustrative, as countries have different domestic institutional arrangements and structures of their financial systems.

The purpose of financial integrity is to deter, defend against, and punish illicit financial activity while facilitating legal financial transactions. A key principle of financial integrity is for AML/CFT frameworks to use a risk-based approach. The international standard for anti-money laundering and countering the financing of terrorism (AML/CFT) is set by the Financial Action Task Force (FATF), which is an inter-governmental body mandated to set standards and promote the effective implementation of the measures to combat money laundering, terrorist financing, proliferation financing, and other related threats to financial integrity. FATF recommends countries follow a risk-based approach to AML/CFT, which entails concentrating AML efforts on where they will be most useful and not using a one-size-fits-all approach. According to FATF, a "risk-based approach includes appropriate strategies to address the full spectrum of risks, from higher to lower risk sectors and entities. Implemented properly, a risk-based approach is more responsive, less burdensome, and delegates more decisions to the people best-placed to make them."

There are several lines of defense against illicit financial activity within the context of a risk-based approach to AML/CFT, as illustrated above. These include: anti-money laundering controls, including Know Your Customer (KYC) compliance and policies, procedures, and controls, from financial institutions and designated non-financial businesses and professions (e.g., casinos, real estate agents, dealers in precious metals and stones, lawyers, notaries, and other independent legal professionals and accountants, trust and company service providers) vis-à-vis their customers (Boxes A and B above); information sharing among financial institutions (see links between Boxes B, C, and D); and suspicious transaction reporting with a centralized and operationally independent Financial Intelligence Unit (FIU, Box E).

The FIU should receive, analyze, and disseminate data on suspicious transactions to law enforcement. The FIU works with domestic financial sector regulators (such as those in the finance ministry and central bank, Box F). FIUs should also share information with other FIUs, through mechanisms such as the Egmont Group of Financial Intelligence Units (see link between Box E and international actors). Together, FIUs and financial regulators cooperate with law enforcement to conduct financial investigations based on information provided by banks and their regulators (Box G). Law enforcement authorities take actions to punish illicit financial activity and are intended to alter the cost–benefit calculus of illicit financial actors and thus deter potential and punish actual financial crimes (see link between Boxes G and A).

Note that the power to undertake supervisory, regulatory, and enforcement activities are shaped by international AML/CFT standards—the FATF's 40 Recommendations (Box H)—as well as other relevant domestic laws, processes, and regulations. If countries fare poorly on their FATF evaluations, they can be "gray listed," or be identified as having strategic AML/CFT deficiencies by FATF. Being gray listed can have implications for the operations of a country's financial system, including for financial stability and access. Hence, there are domestic and international feedback loops within a given polity's AML/CFT regime—chief among them their FATF and FATF-style regional body assessments—which can in turn impact the goals of financial regulatory authorities and financial institutions' access to global markets, such as through correspondent banking relationships.[34] Examples of these feedback loops include financial institutions sharing experiences with regulators to craft regulations on new forms of financial technology, or domestic experience informing international financial regulatory efforts, that can feed back into the polity's laws and regulations.

Source Author and Financial Action Task Force (2021), *Guidance on Risk-Based Supervision* and *Recommendations.*

Annex 2: El Salvador's experience with Bitcoin

This annex provides an overview of Bitcoin in El Salvador. It describes Bitcoin and its underlying distributed ledger technology; provides an analysis of the potential drivers of Bitcoin's price changes; and summarizes the relevant decisions and macroeconomic sectoral implications of Bitcoin adoption. It argues that Bitcoin is not money. Rather, it is a speculative asset that derives its value from reflexive market dynamics in which market

[34] Correspondent banks need to abide by their AML/CFT requirements as set up by their regulators. When attaining correspondent banking relationships, counterparties will look into their respondent banks' AML/CFT preventive measures to ensure that they are not taking derivative undue or unmanaged financial integrity risks through their correspondents.

participants believe that other market participants believe it holds value. In adopting Bitcoin, El Salvador's President Nayib Bukele made a speculative bet on the future value of Bitcoin, which presents several upside and downside risks that El Salvador's authorities will need to manage.

What is Bitcoin? Bitcoin is a cryptographically protected virtual asset, commonly referred to as a "cryptocurrency." Bitcoin transactions are tracked by a peer-to-peer payments system that exists solely on computer networks on a decentralized ledger, or a "blockchain," in which computers operating on the Bitcoin network validate transactions via algorithms. Bitcoin's "distributed ledger technology" (DLT) obviates the need for centralized third parties to validate transactions.[35] Computers produce (or "mine") Bitcoins by solving complex mathematical equations, with the maximum total Bitcoins available to be mined capped at 21 million.[36]

Is Bitcoin money? For Bitcoin to serve as money, it should serve three functions: first, it must be a *unit of account*, or a denomination by which households, firms, and government's price goods, services, assets, and other claims on other economic actors. To date, pricing goods and services in Bitcoin is rare.[37] One potential reason for the lack of use of Bitcoin as a unit of account is its volatility compared to fiat currencies

[35] This distributed ledger technology (DLT) contrasts with the centralized ledger of the traditional banking system, in which transactions are centrally recorded by financial institutions, such as banks. Bouveret and Haksar summarize DLT technology as follows: many cryptocurrencies such as Bitcoin "rely on distributed ledger technology, such as blockchain, to construct a ledger (effectively a database) that is maintained across a network. To ensure that the same cryptocurrency is not spent twice, *each member of the network verifies and validates transactions using technologies derived from computing and cryptography*. Once a decentralized consensus is achieved among members of the network, the transaction is added to the ledger, which is validated. The ledger provides a complete history of the transactions associated with a particular cryptocurrency that is permanent and cannot be manipulated by a single entity. This ability to achieve consensus on the validity of transactions between accounts in a distributed network is a foundational technological shift." For more, see Bouveret and Haksar (2018). Emphasis added.

[36] As argued by Analisa Bala, creating new Bitcoins is energy-intensive: in 2021, Bitcoin mining used more power than the entire country of Denmark, and Bitcoin miners generate about 64 million tons of carbon dioxide annually (comparable to the carbon footprint of Montenegro). For more see Bala (2021). For a good summary of the digital money ecosystem and a taxonomy, see Mancini Griffoli and Adrian (2019).

[37] There are some pilot cases where Bitcoin has been adopted as a unit of account and a medium of exchange, such as the Bitcoin Beach project in the 3,000-person coastal village of El Zonte in El Salvador. The project has faced operational challenges, including

Table 5 Volatility of financial instruments

Instrument	*Average*	*Standard Deviation*	*Coefficient of variation*[a]
Bitcoin	$9,353	13,507	1.44
Turkish Lira	4.795	1.930	0.40
S&P 500	2,728	663	0.24
Gold	$1,393	248	0.18
U.S. headline CPI	249.8	10	0.04
Dollar index	112.7	4.6	0.04

[a]Coefficient of variation found by dividing sample standard deviations by sample averages

Note Sample uses monthly data from October 2014 through September 2021. Instruments are Bitcoin (USD per 1 Bitcoin), the Turkish Lira (Lira per 1 USD), the S&P 500 stock price index (level), spot gold prices per Troy ounce (USD), the trade-weighted U.S. dollar index (level), and the headline U.S. consumer price index (CPI, level)

Source Coindesk, Federal Reserve Economic Data, Author calculations

such as the dollar. For instance, from October 2014 through September 2021, the coefficient of variation of Bitcoin is about eight times higher than the coefficient of variation for gold and about 3.6 times higher than the coefficient of variation for the Turkish Lira—U.S. dollar exchange rate, which is among the most volatile emerging market currencies (see Table 5).

Second, for Bitcoin to serve as money, it should provide a stable *store of value*. While Bitcoin has gained acceptance as an investable asset, it is not yet treated as a stable and safe store of value, as evidenced by the continued popularity of fiat-based savings instruments compared to Bitcoin-based instruments.[38]

ensuring that Bitcoin users have access to necessary technology, such as mobile phones. For more, see BitcoinBeach (2021) and Mak (2021).

[38] Bitcoin enthusiasts often point to the experience of public companies such as Microstrategy, which purchased Bitcoin with its balance sheet cash and has seen its shares outperform common stock indices, as evidence that Bitcoin can serve as a store of value. While Bitcoin's price has increased relative to fiat currencies, large price swings would imply that Bitcoin is not a stable store of value per se. For more on Microstrategy's purchases of Bitcoin, see Microstrategy Incorporated (2021).

Third, to be used as money, Bitcoin must serve as a *medium of exchange*, or a means of settling transactions for goods, services, debt, and assets. While Bitcoin's use as a medium of exchange has gained acceptance on certain use cases (such as for sending remittances across borders), Bitcoin itself may not be the driver of this adoption. Instead, the security and lower cost of DLT relative to traditional payments systems may be driving this use, rather than the Bitcoin unit of account.[39] As argued by Mancini et al., there are few barriers for an electronic version of a fiat currency (e.g., a private "e-dollar" with a fixed exchange rate to fiat currency, such as a dollar-based stablecoin, or a fiat-denominated central bank digital currency) from playing this role on a separate platform, capitalizing on DLT's advantages while not using Bitcoin as the unit of account.[40]

Rather than being money, Bitcoin can instead be thought of as a *speculative asset*. Traditionally, an asset's price should reflect a claim on the income stream of that asset net of costs discounted in present value terms. For example, one method of valuing the equity of publicly listed companies is to forecast dividend-based earnings of the company over a certain period and then to discount those earnings using an appropriate discount rate to arrive at a present value of the stream of net earnings generated by the stock. By design, Bitcoin does not offer such an income stream, nor does Bitcoin's underlying code offer the potential for future earnings on Bitcoin outside of its potential price appreciation against fiat currencies. So traditional valuation methods for fixed income and equity-based securities may not apply to Bitcoin.

[39] Bitcoin's average transaction per second throughput is about 5, compared to 25 for Ethereum, another leading cryptocurrency Villar (2021). While several companies are taking steps to decrease Bitcoin settlement times using second-layer applications such as Lightning Network and Strike, it remains unclear whether Bitcoin itself provides a competitive advantage for serving as a medium of exchange relative to other cryptoassets, notwithstanding improvements in the scalability of Bitcoin. For more on Bitcoin layer two solutions, see Dwyer (2021). Eswar Prasad argues that Bitcoin's environmental footprint and relatively slower transaction speeds, coupled with the low barriers to entry for creating cryptocurrencies that are more environmentally sustainable and faster transacting, pose a risk to Bitcoin, leading Prasad to conclude that "Bitcoin…may not last that much longer." See Shead (2021) and Prasad (2021).

[40] Ibid. For more information on the potential benefits of a central bank digital currency from a U.S.-based perspective, see Baldwin (2021) and Catalini and Massari (2021).

Why, then, has Bitcoin's price risen? As George Soros argues, while market fundamentals drive asset prices, investor perceptions of fundamental value also matter for securities prices and sometimes, prices themselves drive fundamental value. According to Soros, market perceptions are imbricated into market prices, which are *reflexive*. Applying reflexivity to Bitcoin, Soros would argue that Bitcoin has risen in value because market participants believe that other market participants believe it holds value.[41] Any number of justifications for holding Bitcoin can contribute to this reflexive dynamic. For instance, part of the appeal of holding Bitcoin is its limited supply, and investors have likened Bitcoin to a form of "digital gold," which can be used to hedge against currency devaluations brought about by central bank money creation of fiat currencies.[42] Indeed, prima facie evidence indicates a strong correlation between Bitcoin's market value and the total U.S. M2 money supply. For example, one study found that economic impact payments (or COVID-related stimulus checks sent to households in the United States) led to a slight rise in Bitcoin's trading price and volumes, see Divakurani and Zimmerman (2021). Since the first Bitcoins were mined in 2009, the total market capitalization of Bitcoin, or the total number of coins in circulation multiplied by the value of Bitcoin in dollars, has risen to about $900 billion dollars (see Fig. 7).

Why did El Salvador adopt Bitcoin as legal tender? In June 2021, El Salvador's president Nayib Bukele announced that El Salvador would adopt Bitcoin as legal tender, which became effective in September 2021. President Bukele claimed that Bitcoin would help reduce financial transaction fees, especially for cross-border transfers, and enhance financial access.[43] With support from El Salvador's legislature, Bukele mandated that all businesses accept Bitcoin as legal tender and launched an application, Chivo Wallet, to serve as a government-sponsored Bitcoin wallet. To incentivize adoption of Chivo, El Salvador's government gave each citizen about $30 worth of Bitcoin as a sign-on bonus.

What was the reaction to El Salvador's move? According to the *New York Times*, use of Bitcoin in El Salvador has been limited, and "most

[41] Soros (1987).

[42] According to the Chairman of the Federal Reserve Jerome Powell, Bitcoin is a "substitute for gold rather than the dollar" Robb (2021).

[43] DLT can drive down the costs of sending and recording payments, particularly for cross-border transfers.

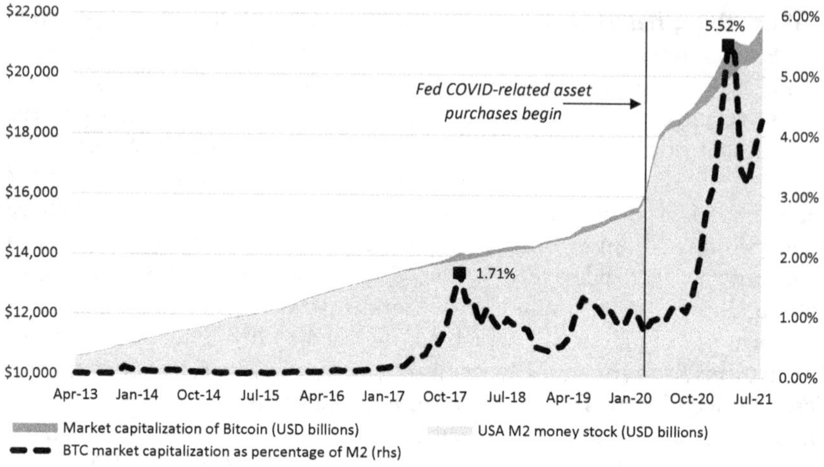

Fig. 7 Bitcoin market capitalization and the United States' M2 money supply (*Source* coinmarketcap.com, Federal Reserve Board of Governors, Author calculations)

[users] fear the cryptocurrency's extreme price volatility, say they lack technological skills or distrust the government's intentions."[44] Bitcoin adoption has also met skepticism from key global stakeholders, including the international financial institutions and rating agencies. Amid reports that El Salvador's authorities approached the World Bank for technical assistance with implementing Bitcoin, a World Bank spokesperson said that this endeavor was "not something the World Bank can support given the environmental and transparency shortcomings" of Bitcoin.[45] Gerry Rice, the IMF's spokesman, said that El Salvador's decision to adopt Bitcoin "raises a number of macroeconomic, financial, and legal issues that require very careful analysis."[46] Moody's, a credit rating agency, found that the move was "credit negative" given the likelihood of Bitcoin adoption hurting the prospects for a deal with the IMF.[47] Others praised El Salvador's move. Leah Wald, CEO of Valkyrie Investments, called

[44] Kurmanaev et al. (2021).

[45] BBC (2021).

[46] Campos and Strohecker (2021).

[47] Rubin (2021).

Bukele's announcement as the "dawn of a new day," with El Salvador setting an example for other countries that are highly dependent on remittances and are trying to tackle financial access issues.[48]

What are El Salvador's plans for a Bitcoin City backed by Bitcoin bonds? In late 2021, Bukele announced plans to build a "Bitcoin City" in Conchagua. Bukele claimed that Bitcoin City would be "fully ecological" and would generate geothermal power from a nearby volcano. Concurrently, El Salvador announced plans to issue $1 billion in "Bitcoin bonds" issued on Liquid, a Bitcoin-based blockchain service. El Salvador plans to use about half of the proceeds of their Bitcoin bonds to purchase Bitcoins in the open market, while the other half will be used to build the infrastructure of Bitcoin City. Ultimately, the payoff structure of the bonds will depend in part on the price performance of Bitcoin over time. If Bitcoin falls in value, then the real debt burden of the Bitcoin bonds will rise, exacerbating debt sustainability risks. If Bitcoin rises in value, then the assets purchased by Bitcoin bonds will reduce the debt service burden associated with Bitcoin bonds. Bukele claimed that depending on the price performance of Bitcoin, bond holders could receive a special price dividend.[49]

What are the implications of having a dual dollar and Bitcoin-based monetary system? By investing its foreign exchange reserves into Bitcoin, El Salvador taken a directional view on the price performance of Bitcoin relative to the dollar, essentially turning the management of its foreign exchange reserves into a cryptocurrency investment fund.[50] Bitcoin City and Bitcoin bonds represent a wager by Bukele that Bitcoin will continue to rise in value and that specializing in Bitcoin production and speculation can be a durable comparative advantage for El Salvador, anchored by El Salvador's being a first mover in this space.

[48] Maki and Hajric (2021).

[49] Kharpal (2021). See PYMNTS.com (2022) for more on regulatory changes undertaken by El Salvador to create a legal framework for issuing cryptoassets. For an interview with Samsom Mow, Chief Strategy Officer of Blockstream, a company advising El Salvador on its Bitcoin bonds, see Morris (2021).

[50] Goschenko (2021). Since El Salvador's early Bitcoin purchases, the value of Bitcoin relative to the dollar has increased about 50%. In October 2021, Nayib Bukele announced that *Fidebitcoin*, El Salvador's Bitcoin trust, would use some of its Bitcoin profits to fund veterinary hospitals in the country.

What are the policy implications of Bitcoin adoption? It will be important for El Salvador to ensure that its dual exchange rate standard does not compromise macroeconomic and financial stability, market access, and financial integrity while offering advantages relative to other technology-enabled payments systems, such as stablecoins. Speculating with foreign exchange reserves and El Salvador's sovereign balance sheet could justify these risks if Bitcoin continues to rise in value, Bitcoin City reaches its full potential, and the reputational risks of Bitcoin adoption are well managed. On the other hand, should Bitcoin underperform or should Bitcoin adoption raise perceptions of the riskiness of El Salvador as a financial jurisdiction, then El Salvador's wager could backfire, creating significant fiscal, external, and real economy stresses on the country. These potential sectoral implications of El Salvador's adoption of Bitcoin are summarized briefly in Table 6.

Table 6 Sectoral implications and considerations of Bitcoin adoption in El Salvador

Real sector	• Opportunity to be a "first mover" specializing in the adoption of Bitcoin as a legal tender, including positive reputational effects among digital money-enthusiast investors and specializing in services in the digital asset space • Lower transactions costs of cross-border remittances could raise household income, leading to permanent welfare gains and higher domestic absorption • Dutch Disease effects if resources diverted into Bitcoin mining and other Bitcoin infrastructure fall in value • Carbon footprint may rise depending on the method of Bitcoin mining
Fiscal sector	• Potential for market access challenges given higher borrowing costs amid credit ratings actions due to Bitcoin adoption • Bitcoin adoption may lead to greater formalization if the Bitcoin economy is co-opted into the formal economy • May lead to the development of a parallel transactions system that incentivizes tax avoidance • Contingent liability risks of operational losses at *Fidebitcoin*, especially in an adverse Bitcoin price scenario that would lead to dollar-based recapitalization needs

(continued)

Table 6 (continued)

Monetary sector	• Move from single (i.e., dollar-based) to dual currency system fixed exchange rate regime • Depending on domestic and global adoption rates, swings in the dollar-Bitcoin exchange rate can impact competitiveness and monetary stability (for instance, amid high adoption rates, a surge in Bitcoin's price relative to the dollar could lead to overheating and inflation, while a Bitcoin crash could trigger wealth losses, growth falling below potential, and deflation) • There will be a need for Bitcoin-denominated loss provisions to enable critical monetary policy functions, such as smoothing global capital flows (particularly those denominated in Bitcoin) and serving as a lender of last resort should financial sector liabilities become increasingly denominated in Bitcoin
Financial sector	• Adoption of Bitcoin could lead to financial disintermediation risks as savers convert dollar holdings to Bitcoin held in Bitcoin wallets • Can create currency mismatches among financial institutions if Bitcoin-based liabilities rise in real terms relative to dollar-based assets, reducing dollar-based equity and leading to funding stress • Heightened perceptions of El Salvador being a risky financial system due to Bitcoin adoption could create correspondent banking relationship pressures and generate risks to global financial access. Greater risks of money laundering vulnerabilities as El Salvador becomes a hub for Bitcoin trading
External sector	• Bitcoin adoption could create an impetus for greater foreign inflows as El Salvador becomes a larger source of dollar-Bitcoin liquidity to global markets. Higher inflows could lead to higher domestic prices (in both dollars and Bitcoin), leading to a real exchange rate appreciation and reduced competitiveness • Perceptions of financial risks could lead to capital dollar outflows as savers seek the safety of non-Bitcoin-based financial systems. Challenged relationships with international financial institutions due to Bitcoin adoption could make it difficult to deal with periods of acute funding stress • Specialization in Bitcoin mining and financial technology could anchor a comparative advantage in frontier technology financial services if risks are appropriately managed

Source Author

References

Adrian, T., Erceg, C., Gray, S., & Sahay, R. (2021). Asset purchases and direct financing: Guiding principles for emerging markets and developing economies during COVID-19 and beyond. *Monetary and Capital Markets Department Departmental Papers Series* (023), 1–49.

Akitoby, B. (2018, March). Raising revenue: Five country cases illustrate how best to improve tax collection. *Finance & Development*, 18–21.
Baer, W., & Montes-Rojas, G. (2010). From privatization to re-nationalization: What went wrong with privatizations in Argentina? *Review of International Political Economy, 36*(3), 323–337.
Bala, A. (2021, September). Cleaning up crypto. *Finance & Development*, 68–69.
Baldwin, R. (2021). *The promises and perils of central bank digital currencies.* U.S. House Financial Services Committee Subcommittee on National Security, International Development and Monetary Policy. Retrieved from U.S. House Financial Services Committee Subcommittee on National Security, International Development and Monetary Policy.
BBC. (2021, June 17). *World Bank rejects El Salvador request for Bitcoin help.* BBC.com. Retrieved November 1, 2021, from https://www.bbc.com/news/business-57507386
Beckers, F., & Stegemann, U. (2021). *A smarter way to think about public–private partnerships.* McKinsey & Company. https://www.mckinsey.com/business-functions/risk-and-resilience/our-insights/a-smarter-way-to-think-about-public-private-partnerships
Bergman, M. (2010). *Tax evasion and the rule of law in Latin America: The political culture of cheating and compliance in Argentina and Chile.* The Pennsylvania State University Press.
BitcoinBeach. (2021). *Our work is just getting started.* Retrieved November 1, 2021, from https://www.bitcoinbeach.com/#about
Bouveret, A., & Haksar, V. (2018). What are cryptocurrencies? *Finance & Development, 55*(2), 26–27.
Call, C. (2020a). *Legacies & lessons of hybrid anti-impunity missions in Central America.* American University. Retrieved November 2, 2021, from https://www.american.edu/centers/latin-american-latino-studies/lessons-legacies-hybrid-anti-impunity-missions.cfm
Call, C. (2020b). Fleeting success: The legacy of Honduras' international anti-corruption mission. *CLALS Working Paper Series* (27), 1–64.
Call, C. (2020c). Too much success? The legacy and lessons of the international commission against impunity in Guatemala. *CLALS Working Paper Series*, 1–106.
Campos, R., & Strohecker, K. (2021, June 10). *IMF sees legal, economic issues with El Salvador's bitcoin move.* Retrieved October 10, 2021, from https://www.reuters.com/business/finance/imf-sees-legal-economic-issues-with-el-salvador-bitcoin-move-2021-06-10/
Catalini, C., & Massari, J. (2021, August 10). Stablecoins and the future of money. *Harvard Business Review*. Retrieved October 30, 2021, from https://hbr.org/2021/08/stablecoins-and-the-future-of-money

Chamon, M., Hofman, D., Magud, E. N., & Werner, A. (2019). *Foreign exchange intervention in inflation targeters in Latin America*. International Monetary Fund.

Charumilind, S., Craven, M., Lamb, J., Singhal, S., & Wilson, M. (2021, October 28). *Pandemic to endemic: How the world can learn to live with COVID-19*. McKinsey & Company. Retrieved November 13, 2021, from https://www.mckinsey.com/industries/healthcare-systems-and-services/our-insights/pandemic-to-endemic-how-the-world-can-learn-to-live-with-covid-19

Cohen, C., Ali Abbas, S., Anthony, M., Best, T., Breuer, P., Miao, H., … Togo, E. (2020). The role of state-contingent debt instruments in sovereign debt restructurings. *IMF Staff Discussion Note*, 1–34.

Colvin, C., & Fliers, P. (2020, May 21). *How the US government seized all citizens' gold in 1930s*. The Conversation https://theconversation.com/how-the-us-government-seized-all-citizens-gold-in-1930s-138467

Cook, T. R. (2011). The financial arm of the FARC: A threat finance perspective. *Journal of Strategic Security, 4*(1), 19–36.

Corden, W. M. (2002). *Too sensational: On the choice of exchange rate regimes*. MIT Press.

De Gregorio, J. (2019). *Inflation targets in Latin America, 19*(19), 1–16.

DeCambre, M. (2021, March 27). *Bitcoin could become 'outlawed the way gold was outlawed' in 1934, speculates Bridgewater's Dalio*. MarketWatch. Retrieved October 26, 2021, from https://www.marketwatch.com/story/bitcoin-could-become-outlawed-the-way-gold-was-outlawed-in-1934-speculates-bridgewaters-dalio-11616603781

Dell'Ariccia, G., Ferreira, C., Jenkinson, N., Laeven, L., Martin, A., Minoiu, C., & Popov, A. (2018). Managing the sovereign-bank nexus. *European Central Bank Working Paper Series* (2177), 1–57.

Divakurani, A., & Zimmerman, P. (2021). Uncovering retail trading in bitcoin: The impact of COVID-19 stimulus checks. *Federal Reserve Bank of Cleveland Working Papers, 21*(13), 1–79.

Dussauge Laguna, M. I. (2011). The challenges of implementing merit-based personnel policies in Latin America: Mexico's civil service reform experience. *Journal of Comparative Policy Analysis: Research and Practice, 13*(1), 51–73.

Dwyer, K. (2021, September). *What are cryptocurrency layer 2 scaling solutions?* Coinmarketcap.com. Retrieved November 11, 2021, from https://coinmarketcap.com/alexandria/article/what-are-cryptocurrency-layer-2-scaling-solutions

Egmont Group. (2018). *Co-chairs' statement 25th plenary of the Egmont group of financial intelligence units*. Egmont Group.

Fernández, J. W. (2019). More aid won't stop Central America's migrant crisis: What U.S. aid can and can't achieve in the Northern Triangle. *Foreign Affairs*.

Feyen, E., & Zuccardi, I. (2019). The Sovereign-Bank Nexus in EMDEs: What is it, is it rising, and what are its policy implications? *The World Bank Policy Research Working Paper Series* (8950), 1–52.

Force, F. A. T. (2014). *Virtual currencies: Key definitions and potential AML/CFT risks*. Financial Action Task Force.

Force, F. A. T. (2019). *Guidance for a risk-based approach to virtual assets and virtual asset service providers*. Financial Action Task Force.

Fitch Ratings. (2021, May 5). *Rating action commentary: Fitch affirms Guatemala at 'BB-'; outlook stable*. Fitch Ratings. https://www.fitchratings.com/research/sovereigns/fitch-affirms-guatemala-at-bb-outlook-stable-05-05-2021

FitchRatings. (2021). *Bitcoin could increase regulatory, AML risks for El Salvador Banks*. FitchRatings.

Forni, L., & Escolano, J. (2014). *Public employment and compensation reform during times of fiscal consolidation, 14*(192), 1–23.

Goodhart, C., & Pradhan, M. (2020). *The great demographic reversal: Ageing societies, waning inequality, and an inflation revival*. Palgrave Macmillan.

Gopinath, G. (2020, October). *A long, uneven and uncertain ascent*. IMFBlog. Retrieved November 1, 2021, from https://blogs.imf.org/2020/10/13/a-long-uneven-and-uncertain-ascent/

Goschenko, S. (2021, October 11). *Salvadoran President Nayib Bukele announces construction of vet hospital with bitcoin trust funds*. Retrieved October 30, 2021, from https://news.bitcoin.com/salvadoran-president-nayib-bukele-announces-construction-of-vet-hospital-with-bitcoin-trust-funds/

Hashimoto, H., Mooi, Y., Pedras, G., Roy, A., Chung, K., Galeza, T., … Paladines, C. (2021). Guidance note for developing government local currency bond markets. *International Monetary Fund and the World Bank*, 1–157.

Heller, P. (2005). Back to basics—Fiscal space: What it is and how to get it. *Finance and Development, 42*(2).

International Monetary Fund. (2017, October). *The IMF and the fight against money laundering and the financing of terrorism*. International Monetary Fund Factsheet. http://www.imf.org/external/np/exr/facts/aml.htm

International Monetary Fund. (2018). *Assessing fiscal space: An update and stocktaking*. International Monetary Fund.

International Monetary Fund. (2019a). Fourth progress report on inclusion of enhanced contractual provisions in international sovereign bond contracts. *IMF Policy Papers*, 1–12.

International Monetary Fund. (2019b). *IMF policy paper: A strategy for IMF engagement on social spending*. International Monetary Fund.

International Monetary Fund. (2020). *Regional economic outlook: Western Hemisphere*. International Monetary Fund.

International Monetary Fund. (2021a). *Guatemala: 2021 Article IV Consultation—Press release; staff report; and statement by the Executive Director for Guatemala*. International Monetary Fund.

International Monetary Fund. (2021b). *Honduras: Fourth reviews under the stand-by arrangement and the arrangement under the standby credit facility, requests for augmentation of access, extension and rephasing of the arrangements, and waivers of nonobservance of performance criteria*. International Monetary Fund.

Keynes, J. M. (1931). *Essays in persuasion*. Macmillan.

Kharpal, A. (2021, November 22). *El Salvador plans to create a 'bitcoin city' and raise $1 billion via a 'bitcoin bond'*. CNBC. Retrieved January 3, 2022, from https://www.cnbc.com/2021/11/22/el-salvador-plans-bitcoin-city-raise-1-billion-via-bitcoin-bond.html

Krueger, A. (2002). *A new approach to sovereign debt restructuring*. International Monetary Fund.

Krueger, A., & Hagan, S. (2005). Sovereign workouts: An IMF perspective. *Chicago Journal of International Law, 6*(1), 203–218.

Kurmanaev, A., Avelar, B., & Livni, E. (2021, October 7). Bitcoin preaches financial liberty. A strongman is testing that promise. *The New York Times*.

Lanau, S., & Roldos, J. (2017). *The growth return of infrastructure in Latin America*. International Monetary Fund Working Papers.

Lipschitz, L., & Schadler, S. (2019). *Macroeconomics for professionals: A guide for analysts and those who need to understand them*. Cambridge University Press.

Liu, Y., & Mao, J. (2019). How do tax incentives affect investment and productivity? Firm-level evidence from China. *American Economic Journal: Economic Policy, 11*(3), 261–291.

Mak, A. (2021, June 16). *What happened when a 3,000-person village in El Salvador became "bitcoin beach"*. Slate.com. Retrieved November 1, 2021, from https://slate.com/technology/2021/06/el-zonte-el-salvador-bitcoin-beach-legal-tender.html

Maki, S., & Hajric, V. (2021, June 13). *Wall Street asks if bitcoin can ever replace fiat currencies*. Bloomberg. Retrieved November 1, 2021, from https://www.bloomberg.com/news/articles/2021-06-13/wall-street-asks-if-bitcoin-can-ever-replace-fiat-currencies

Mancini Griffoli, T., & Adrian, T. (2019). The rise of digital money. *IMF Fintech Notes*, 1056.

Microstrategy Incorporated. (2021, February 12). *Form 10-K*. 2021: Securities and Exchange Commission.

Morris, D. Z. (2021, December 16). *Behind the scenes of El Salvador's bitcoin bond with the man who designed it: Samson Mow reveals the fast-moving process behind a radical financial experiment.* CoinDesk. https://www.coindesk.com/layer2/2021/12/16/behind-the-scenes-of-el-salvadors-bitcoin-bond-with-the-man-who-designed-it/

Muzinich, J. (2021). America's crypto conundrum: Protecting security without crushing innovation. *Foreign Affairs, 100*(6), 129–141.

Nizam, R., Zulkefly, A. K., Rahman, A. A., & Sarmidi, T. (2020). Financial inclusiveness and economic growth: New evidence using a threshold regression analysis. *Economic Research, 33*(1), 1465–1484.

Omar, N., & Hajudin, H. (2015, February). FATF recommendations related to DNFBPs on anti money laundering assessment. *Journal of Economics, Business and Management, 3*(2), 156–160.

Ortiz, I., Cummins, M., & Karunanethy, K. (2017). *Fiscal space for social protection and the SDGs: Options to expand social investments in 187 countries.* Extension of Social Security Working Paper.

Prasad, E. (2021). *The future of money: How the digital revolution is transforming currencies and finance.* The Belknap Press of Harvard University Press.

Purcell, J., & Rossi, I. (2019). Privacy vs. transparency: Countries must strike the right balance as they combat illicit financial flows. *Finance & Development, 56*(3), 18–21.

PYMNTS.com. (2022, January 9). Retrieved January 13, 2022, from https://www.pymnts.com/blockchain/bitcoin/2022/el-salvador-regulatory-regime-for-bitcoin-volcano-bonds-as-soon-as-february/

Richardson, G., Komai, A., & Gou, M. (2013, November 22). *Gold Reserve Act of 1934.* Federal Reserve History. https://www.federalreservehistory.org/essays/gold-reserve-act

Robb, G. (2021, March 22). *Fed's Powell says bitcoin is more of a substitute for gold than the dollar.* MarketWatch. Retrieved October 30, 2021, from https://www.marketwatch.com/story/feds-powell-says-bitcoin-is-more-of-a-substitute-for-gold-than-the-dollar-11616424786

Roldos, J., David, A., Perez, C., & Pienknagura, S. (2019). *Regional economic outlook: Western Hemisphere, labor market dynamics and informality over the business cycle in LAC.* Western Hemisphere Department. International Monetary Fund.

Rubin, J. (2021, July 30). *Moody's lowers El Salvador rating, maintains negative outlook partly due to bitcoin law.* Yahoo.com. Retrieved November 1, 2021, from https://www.yahoo.com/now/moody-lowers-el-salvador-rating-005830979.html

Sabet, D. M. (2020). When corruption funds the political system: A case study of Honduras. *Woodrow Wilson Center*, 1–49.

Sahay, R., Eriksson von Allmen, U., Lahreche, A., Khera, P., Ogawa, S., Bazarbash, M., & Beaton, K. (2020). The promise of Fintech: Financial inclusion in the post COVID-19 era. *IMF Departmental Paper Series* (20/09), 1–83.

Savoy, C. M., & Sady-Kennedy, T. A. (2021, September). *Economic opportunity in the Northern Triangle: U.S. government support for private sector-led development*. Center for Strategic and International Studies.

Schneider, A. (2012). *State-building and tax regimes in Central America*. Cambridge University Press.

Schwarz, N., Chen, K., Poh, K., Jackson, G., Kao, K., Fernando, F., & Markevych, M. (2021a). *Virtual assets and anti-money laundering and combating the financing of terrorism (1): Some legal and practical considerations*. International Monetary Fund.

Schwarz, N., Chen, K., Poh, K., Jackson, G., Kao, K., Fernando, F., & Markevych, M. (2021b). *Virtual assets and anti-money laundering and combating the financing of terrorism (2): Effective anti-money laundering and combating the financing of terrorism regulatory and supervisory framework—Some legal and practical considerations*. International Monetary Fund.

Seligman, L. (2019). *The hidden driver: Climate change and migration in Central America's northern triangle*. American Security Project.

Shead, S. (2021, December 17). *Bitcoin 'may not last that much longer,' academic warns.* CNBC. https://www.cnbc.com/2021/12/17/bitcoin-may-not-last-that-much-longer-academic-warns.html

Sobel, M. (2016). Strengthening collective action clauses: Catalysing change-the back story. *Capital Markets Law Journal, 11*(1), 3–11.

Soros, G. (1987). *The alchemy of finance*. Wiley.

Stolper, A. E., & Dougherty, S. (2017). Collective action clauses: How the Argentina litigation changed the sovereign debt markets. *Capital Markets Law Journal, 12*(2), 1–14.

Swiston, A. (2011). Official dollarization as a monetary regime: Its effects on el Salvador. *IMF Working Paper*, 1–26.

Taylor, C., Wilson, C., Holttinen, E., & Morozova, A. (2019). *Institutional arrangements for Fintech regulation and supervision*. International Monetary Fund.

The World Bank. (2020, October 29). *Remittance prices worldwide: Making markets more transparent*. Worldbank.org. https://remittanceprices.worldbank.org/en/corridor/United-States/El-Salvador?start_date=1601524800&end_date=1609477199

Ubide, Á., & Levy Yeyati, E. (2015, February 19). *GDP-linked bonds: Can Argentina's failure become Greece's success?* Peterson Institute for International Economics. Retrieved January 3, 2022, from https://www.piie.com/blogs/realtime-economic-issues-watch/gdp-linked-bonds-can-argentinas-failure-become-greeces-success

United States Department of State. (2021). *International narcotics control strategy report*. Bureau of International Narcotics and Law Enforcement Affairs.

Villar, T. (2021, August 3). *Bitcoin is slow: what is the fastest cryptocurrency?* MUD.com. Retrieved November 1, 2021, from https://www.makeuseof.com/bitcoin-is-slow-what-is-the-fastest-cryptocurrency/

Weyland, K. (2004). *The politics of market reform in fragile democracies: Argentina, Brazil, Peru, and Venezuela*. Princeton University Press.

World Bank. (2014, June 30). *World Bank issues its first ever catastrophe bond linked to natural hazard risks in sixteen Caribbean countries*. The World Bank. https://www.worldbank.org/en/news/press-release/2014/06/30/world-bank-issues-its-first-ever-catastrophe-bond-linked-to-natural-hazard-risks-in-sixteen-caribbean-countries

World Bank. (2015). *Global financial development report 2015/2016: Long-term finance*. Global Financial Development Report. World Bank.

World Bank. (2021). *IBRD funding program*. Capital at Risk Notes. https://treasury.worldbank.org/en/about/unit/treasury/ibrd/ibrd-capital-at-risk-notes#3

Yilla, K., & Liang, N. (2020, February 11). *What are macroprudential tools?* Brookings. https://www.brookings.edu/blog/up-front/2020/02/11/what-are-macroprudential-tools/#cancel

CHAPTER 3

Enhancing Global Engagement

Abstract This chapter describes how external stakeholders, including the United States, Canada, Mexico, the private sector, civil society, and international financial institutions can help the Northern Triangle countries enact the economic reforms identified in this book. The United States' strategic interests in the Northern Triangle include maintaining influence in the Western Hemisphere, limiting adverse spillovers from the region, and promoting democratic values and prosperity. These interests are best met by adopting a series of pragmatic principles of engagement in the region, which this chapter outlines. Canada and Mexico have an interest in enhancing governance in the Northern Triangle because adverse spillovers from the region can have impact on their relations with the United States. The private sector and civil society can be leveraged to achieve consensus and cohesion in policy reform, while the international financial institutions can offer unique areas of expertise that can benefit the Northern Triangle countries. The chapter concludes by noting that while sustained multilateral action to assist the Northern Triangle can help them escape their governance traps, strong domestic political ownership and genuine public calls for enhanced governance and accountability will ultimately decide whether reform efforts succeed or fail.

Keywords Canadian foreign policy · Global cooperation and governance reform · International financial institutions and the Northern

N. Shenai, *Escaping the Governance Trap*,
https://doi.org/10.1007/978-3-030-99023-7_3

Triangle · Mexican foreign policy · United States' strategic interests in the Northern Triangle

The first two chapters of *Escaping the Governance Trap* provided a framework for understanding the development challenges facing the Northern Triangle countries of El Salvador, Guatemala, and Honduras. Chapter 1 argued that these countries were stuck in a "governance trap," which this book defines as *a path-dependent equilibrium in which weak states with contested authority fail to penetrate civil society and achieve self-sustaining economic growth, resulting in states that under supply political order and economic opportunity*. Chapter 2 identified several economic reforms that could help the Northern Triangle countries escape their governance traps. It claimed that fiscal reform, well-calibrated monetary and exchange rate policy, financial sector policy (specifically related to enhanced financial access and integrity), and structural reforms could increase fiscal space and resilience, strengthen macroeconomic and financial stability, improve financial access and deterrence, and boost potential growth.

The purpose of this chapter is to build on the theoretical and economic arguments advanced in Chapters 1 and 2 to explain how global partners, including stakeholders such as the United States, Canada, Mexico, civil society, the private sector, and international institutions can help the Northern Triangle countries by supporting the previously identified reform priorities. The premise of this chapter is that the scale of the challenges facing the Northern Triangle countries is large, and therefore international partners' support could help close capacity gaps and strengthen the political will to reform.[1] But foreign support alone cannot compensate for a lack of national ownership of reform efforts. This chapter situates each stakeholder within the context of its strategic interests in the Northern Triangle and identifies several principles of engagement that follow from these interests.[2]

[1] Foreign support can compensate for a lack of domestic will or capacity to reform by changing the incentives of the region's political leaders. Timely aid flows and technical assistance can help with capacity building as well or address near-term fiscal risks while promoting macroeconomic adjustment.

[2] Note that this chapter takes as given the United States' immigration and drug enforcement policies. While changes to these policies may impact bilateral relationships between

1 The United States

Since the nineteenth century, the United States has tried to preserve its influence, take advantage of economic opportunities, and project power in the Western Hemisphere. This policy emerged in the decades following the founding of the United States and continued during both World Wars and the Cold War, through the fall of the Soviet Union and into the present day. The intensity and proactiveness of U.S. engagement in Latin America has ebbed and flowed, with Latin America policy at times becoming a core foreign policy priority (such as during the turn of the twentieth century, early 1960s, or the 2010s), while at other times being subsumed by other foreign policy priorities, including after the September eleventh terrorist attacks. Although U.S. focus on Latin America has been sporadic, the United States is often compelled to act when it perceives its core interests are at stake in the region, including when the region may be at risk of falling into the sphere of influence of other great powers. With the continued flow of outbound migration from Central America and the rise of China's involvement in the region, there are good reasons to expect the United States will continue to be pulled back into the Northern Triangle and forced to grapple with the region's governance issues.[3]

In 1823, U.S. President James Monroe issued the Monroe Doctrine, which asserted that Europeans should not take new colonies in the Western Hemisphere and committed the United States to a policy of non-interference in Europe. By foreswearing U.S. involvement in Europe in exchange for European non-interference in the Western Hemisphere, Monroe elevated the Western Hemisphere as a strategically important

the United States and the Northern Triangle countries, drug policy and immigration reform remain politically contested, with policy breakthroughs uncertain.

[3] For a few recent volumes on China's economic engagement in Latin America, including its overseas lending and impact on governance in debtor countries, see Kaplan (2021) and Wise (2020).

region to the United States (Zoellick, 2020, 60–63).[4] In 1904, U.S. President Theodore Roosevelt issued a Corollary to the Monroe Doctrine that stated that the United States had the right to intervene in the Western Hemisphere to exercise an "international police power" to defend U.S. economic interests and restore political order in the United States' near abroad (Dobson & Marsh, 2006, 7).[5] European involvement in the Western Hemisphere contributed partially to the United States' decision to enter World War I (1914–1918) against Germany, after the United States intercepted a message from Germany urging Mexico to join the war effort against the United States. This message, known as the Zimmermann Telegram, helped President Woodrow Wilson make his case for U.S. involvement in the war to the U.S. Congress and to the American people, culminating in the United States joining World War I on the Allies' side in April 1917 (Zoellick, 2020, 159–162). The Great Depression and World War II (1929–1945) saw a thaw in U.S.–Latin American relations, with the United States pursing a Good Neighbor policy of non-intervention in Latin America and aligning with Mexico during World War II (Beck, 2007).[6]

The United States pivoted from President Franklin Roosevelt's Good Neighbor policy during the Cold War. Intent on maintaining access to the Panama Canal, ensuring military hegemony in the Caribbean Basin, and containing the spread of communism, the United States returned

[4] President James Monroe issued the Monroe Doctrine in response to threats of the European Holy Alliance of Austria, Prussia, and Russia to support absolutist regimes, including the Western Hemisphere, while recognizing the threat posed to the U.S. homeland from European expansion from strong European colonies. Despite the historic and aspirational significance of the Monroe Doctrine, analysts have shown that the Monroe Doctrine had little practical effect until the turn of the twentieth century. For instance, the United States demurred from providing assistance to newly independent states in the Western Hemisphere and did nothing when Great Britain declared present-day Belize a British colony in 1862, see Kupchan (2020, 113–116).

[5] According to former U.S. Secretary of State Henry Kissinger, Roosevelt's Corollary to the Monroe Doctrine reflected Roosevelt's realization that the United States could no longer rely on hemispheric isolation to guarantee its security. Therefore, establishing a more muscular foreign policy in the Western Hemisphere (with greater latitude to intervene in the domestic affairs of countries in the region) was critical to preserving American security by promoting political order and governments that were perceived as favorable to U.S. interests (Kissinger, 1994, 38–39).

[6] It is worth noting that World War II dynamics in Latin America cut both ways, with the United States growing closer to Mexico and Brazil, on one hand, while distancing itself from Argentina.

to a more activist foreign policy toward Latin America.[7] During the Cold War, the United States intervened in the domestic politics throughout the hemisphere. For instance, in 1954 the United States Central Intelligence Agency (CIA) orchestrated a coup d'état against Guatemalan President Jacobo Árbenz, replacing him with a military dictatorship led by the authoritarian Carlos Castillo Armas (Dobson & Marsh, 2006, 84–85).[8] The pattern established by the Guatemala coup recurred throughout the Cold War, including in interventions with varying degrees of success in Cuba (1961), the Dominican Republic (1965), Chile (1973), Nicaragua (throughout the 1980s), Grenada (1983), Panama (1989), and Haiti (1994) (Dobson & Marsh, 2006, xxi–xvi).

The United States supported regional initiatives to promote security and inter-American cooperation during the Cold War, including via the Inter-American Treaty of Reciprocal Assistance (known as the Rio Treaty) of 1947 and the Organization of American States (OAS), the world's oldest regional multilateral organization, in 1948. The Rio Military Pact stipulated that an attack on one country in the hemisphere was an attack on all, while the OAS provided a forum for settling disputes and promoting hemispheric economic and social development (Tomasek, 1959). Presidents John F. Kennedy and Ronald Reagan launched economic initiatives to complement these military and political efforts, known as the Alliance for Progress (1961) and Caribbean Basin Initiative (1982), respectively. The Alliance for Progress, a widely remembered program, provided transfers and loans to support economic development and faster per-capita income growth, land reform, and ultimately more republican governments, with the hope that this assistance

[7] See Ellis (2020) for a summary on China's recent forays into the Caribbean, including a synopsis of U.S. interests in the region. On how previous eras of great power rivalry impacted Latin America, see B. Smith (2008). Smith also provides a good framing of U.S. policy toward Latin America during the post-9/11 unipolar moment.

[8] U.S. policymakers in the Eisenhower Administration feared that Árbenz was a communist sympathizer, had the backing of communists worldwide including the Soviet Union, and intended to threaten U.S. economic interests in Guatemala via land reform and expropriation of about a quarter of a million acres in land from the Boston-based United Fruit Company. Officials thought that Árbenz may have been planning to use Guatemala's strategic location to threaten vital U.S. interests in Central America, including access to the U.S.-controlled Panama Canal (David, 1987). Skidmore et al. claim that the 1954 Guatemala coup "marked a turning point in Guatemalan history," as it "eliminated the forces of the political center" and entrenched a governing alliance between landlords, foreign investors, and right-wing military regimes. See Skidmore et al. (2010, 11).

would make the region more resistant to communist influence and more tightly linked to the United States. The Caribbean Basin Initiative, like the Alliance for Progress, provided preferential economic treatment in exchange for pro-market reforms. While these programs suffered from bureaucratic drift and pushback from vested U.S. domestic interests (such as U.S.-based producers that did not want to compete with foreign products), they signaled a U.S. desire to sway Latin American countries into its economic orbit with a mix of carrots (including development assistance for economic reform) and sticks (i.e., the implicit threat or exercise of military intervention) (Dobson & Marsh, 2006, 90–93).[9]

In the Northern Triangle, the United States had a status quo bias of preserving the existing political order lest these states fall into the Soviet orbit like Cuba and Nicaragua, potentially triggering a wave of refugees from Central America to the United States. Policy toward the region hardened in the 1980s during the administration of President Ronald Reagan, who provided military aid to El Salvador's government to support a counterinsurgency campaign in which nearly 75,000 Salvadorans were killed. The Reagan Administration also used Honduras as a staging ground for anti-Sandinista Nicaraguan forces (the "contras") and sent 3,000 troops to Honduras in 1988 to protect Honduras from an incursion of about 2,000 Sandinistas (Ambrose & Brinkley, 1997, 316–320). William LeoGrande describes Reagan's policy toward Central America as representing "a Manichean struggle between good and evil" (LeoGrande, 1990, 595). He finds that during the Reagan years, "Central America became a symbol and test case for demonstrating Reagan's new hard line against international communism" (LeoGrande, 1998, xi). Still, this activist policy created considerable domestic backlash, including from the U.S. Congress.

Following the fall of the Soviet Union, U.S. foreign policy toward Latin America and the Northern Triangle shifted from the narrow pursuit of anti-communism to a more discerning approach that prioritized trade and economic growth, multilateral cooperation, and democratization.

[9] Indeed, coupled with the United States' support for debt treatments and macroeconomic stabilization programs during the Latin America debt crisis of the 1980s, these efforts indicate that U.S. involvement in Latin America did not exclusively grow out of the barrel of a gun but instead had multiple facets that spanned economic, social, and political engagement. For a good summary on the 1980s Latin American debt crisis and the U.S. role, see Sims and Romero (2013).

In 1991, the OAS adopted the "Santiago Commitment to Democracy and the Renewal of the Inter-American System." The Santiago Declaration committed OAS member states to take a more active role in the promotion of democracy, free markets, and inter-American cooperation, which later included commitments to support democratically elected governments that were threatened to be overthrown by force, including military coups (Dobson & Marsh, 2006, 186–187; Schnably, 1994). With support from the United States, in 1992 El Salvador's government and the rebels represented by the Farabundo Martí National Liberation Front (FMLN) signed a peace agreement and agreed to democratic participation, ending El Salvador's civil conflict. Guatemala's civil war also ended in the 1990s. The United States agreed to free trade pacts with Canada and Mexico (the North American Free Trade Agreement) in 1994 and with Central America and the Dominican Republic (Dominican Republic-Central America Free Trade Agreement) in 2005. Overall, the United States' emphasis on democracy, free markets, and multilateralism in Latin America was representative of the United States' broader push for American values internationally in the wake of the Cold War (Kupchan, 2020, 324–329).

In the 2010s, migration became the preeminent strategic issue in U.S. relations with the Northern Triangle. In 2014, the United States received a surge of unaccompanied minors from Central America at America's Southwest Border. The Obama Administration responded to this influx by adopting a whole-of-government approach to promote economic prosperity and increase security in the Northern Triangle. The U.S. Strategy for Engagement in Central America, building upon the Central America Regional Security Initiative, provided aid and security assistance to the Northern Triangle countries. The Obama Administration also endorsed the Plan of the Alliance for Prosperity in the Northern Triangle, which sought to support strategic economic sectors, invest in human capital, improve public safety, and strengthen transparency and institutions with help from the Inter-American Development Bank. The logic of this approach was clear: the Obama Administration believed that by improving the lives of the citizens in the Northern Triangle via prosperity, better governance (including democracy), and security, it would reduce the drivers of outbound migration (Ernst et al., n.d.; Meyer, 2019). However, the Obama Administration's strategy faced several operational challenges. First, even the best executed strategy to improve governance will likely operate with a lag, particularly when trying to reform norms, customs, and other informal institutions and would require sustained U.S. engagement and adequate and consistent funding. So, even if the strategy targeted the right variables, early results would likely be mixed, and progress would be gradual and not unidirectional. Second, the strategy, by necessity, presumed good faith counterparts in the Northern Triangle willing to undertake reforms that are consistent with U.S. foreign policy goals. While the Northern Triangle countries engaged with the United States and took ownership over their reform agendas, such as through the Alliance for Prosperity, the durability of these reforms—particularly when they threatened vested interests—was lacking.[10] Third, many of the funds tied to the Alliance for Prosperity had structural conditions, which slowed their disbursement. Some conditionality is necessary to safeguard resources, but the lack of domestic consensus and willing partners in the Northern Triangle to meet structural conditions limited the potential impact of these funds (Iesue, 2016).[11] Fourth, flows may have run up against the absorptive capacity of the Northern Triangle countries to receive aid, and fifth, once disbursed, projects may have suffered from imperfect monitoring and impact evaluation.

Following the election of President Donald Trump in 2016, the United States refocused migration efforts with a more aggressive strategy of border enforcement and a more direct approach on U.S. aid to the Northern Triangle, namely that the United States was willing to accept a wider range of domestic policy in exchange for controlling migration. Elected in part due to President Trump's support for increased border security, the Trump Administration adopted as one if its signature issues the construction of a border wall along the U.S.—Mexico border (O'Neil, 2021). The Trump Administration also leaned on third countries to impede migration and to receive asylum seekers and refugees from the Northern Triangle by signing "safe third country" agreements that required migrants to seek asylum in countries other than the United

[10] There have also been reports that domestic security apparatuses have colluded with criminal organizations, rendering security efforts moot due to corruption (Imison, 2016). This problem has bedeviled U.S. security assistance throughout the hemisphere. In Honduras, for example, several former presidents have been accused of involvement in narcotics trafficking (Anderson, 2021). In 2020, the United States arrested a former Mexican defense minister for allegedly protecting drug cartel leaders as well, see Lopez (2021).

[11] See also Kaplan (2021) for how policy conditionality reduces U.S. influence in the region. Kaplan contrasts U.S. policy conditionality with China's "patient" capital approach.

States prior to petitioning for asylum in the United States. The goal of this policy was to deter entry into the United States by asylum seekers to whom, by law, the United States cannot deny entry (Felter & Cheatham, 2019). The Trump Administration also stepped-up enforcement at illegal border crossings, adopting a zero-tolerance policy even for those migrants requesting asylum or traveling with children. Criminal prosecution of adult migrants led to their detention in federal criminal facilities where they could not be accompanied by children. This de facto policy of family separation—impacting some 3,000 children in total—led to considerable public condemnation (Alvarez, 2021).[12] This policy also diverged from the Obama Administration's treatment of illegal entry into the United States as a civil matter (Congressional Research Service, 2018). Finally, in March 2019, the Trump Administration froze about $450 million in programmed foreign aid to the Northern Triangle due to the region's perceived failure at preventing outbound migration (McDonnell, 2019). Although Congress did not agree to some of the Trump Administration's steepest cuts, annual funding for Central America fell from $750 million in FY2017 to about $500 million in FY2021, representing a drop in inflows from about 0.6% to 0.4% of the region's nominal GDP (Meyer, 2021).[13] Overall, Trump's policy sought to pivot to a more muscular migration strategy, relying on stepped up border security and enforcement (including the policy of child separation), a less nuanced approach to the domestic politics of the Northern Triangle countries, less of a focus on the "root causes" of migration, and less tolerance for illegal border crossings, including via so-called "Title 42" expulsions started in March 2020, which allows Customs and Border Protection officers to deny entry into the United States due to the threat of communicable disease (American Immigration Council, 2021).

There were several challenges to this strategy. First, the Trump Administration faced the practical reality that although the United States is a powerful country with influence in the Western Hemisphere, it alone

[12] For a good summary on U.S. detention of child migrants, see Cheatham (2021).

[13] The United States Government Accountability Office found that Northern Triangle foreign assistance funding cuts adversely impacted about 80% of United States Agency for International Development (USAID) projects in that region and about 40% of the Department of State's projects, leading both agencies to report missing performance targets (United States Government Accountability Office, 2021). There are also transactions costs associated with start–stop patterns of aid, as reinstating programs after a suspension takes time and new budgets to reinstate, see Ernst et al. (n.d.).

cannot determine other countries' domestic policies by fiat, particularly when those policies collide with international partners' capacity limitations, lack of political will, or national interests. For instance, under the presidency of Andrés Manuel López Obrador, Mexico refused to sign a "safe third country" agreement with the United States.[14] Although the Northern Triangle countries agreed with the Trump Administration request to process asylum seekers, these countries lacked the infrastructure to process tens of thousands of asylum cases (Felter & Cheatham, 2019; Ibe, 2020). Second, the Trump Administration's strategy did not address the "root causes" of migration, specifically the Northern Triangle's governance vulnerabilities. While more defensive border security measures may be useful tactics in a strategy of optimizing between short-term domestic political imperatives (i.e., responding to public pressure on migration), broad international interests, and strategic interactions with the Northern Triangle governments, and might have some deterrence value, heavy-handed threats such as withdrawing aid will ultimately prove self-defeating in efforts to address outbound migration. Moreover, actually suspending aid disrupts effective assistance programs, entrenches pre-existing governance vulnerabilities and economic precarity, and alienates swaths of the Northern Triangle leadership and public opinion, all of which reduces U.S. influence and exacerbates migration challenges. Third, the Trump strategy created domestic backlash in the United States that made achieving a domestic political consensus for commonsense solutions to migration more elusive. Polls conducted in 2018 showed that voting-age adults in the United States opposed child separation by a margin of almost three-to-one (Mehta, 2018). Wallace and Millán find that the most ardent supporters of draconian migration policy, including child separation, discontinuing Temporary Protected Status for various groups, and constructing a border wall tended to be motivated by perceptions of cultural threats and identity vulnerability (Wallace & Zepeda-Millán, 2020). By crafting a policy for a vocal minority of the electorate, the Trump Administration put achieving a domestic consensus on migration policy further out of reach, which undermines the continuity of policies and efforts to solve security challenges.

Since taking office in January 2021, President Joseph Biden has restored several Obama-era migration policies while curtailing many of

[14] That said, López Obrador's government has been somewhat pliant on U.S. migration policy in some respects, including by facilitating the "Remain in Mexico" program.

President Trump's more heavy-handed policies, including the construction of the border wall and child separation, though a full rollback of policies has been difficult to achieve or not pursued in some cases.[15] However, the broad U.S. strategy for addressing migration has changed significantly. A centerpiece of the Biden agenda is addressing the "root causes" of migration. Pillars of this approach include improving economic security, combating corruption, promoting liberal values (including human rights and freedom of the press), and countering violence, with a focus on sexual, gender-based, and domestic violence (National Security Council, 2021). The House of Representatives agreed to grant the first tranche of a four-year aid package to the Northern Triangle ($866 million out of $4 billion pledged over four years), with an emphasis on tackling public corruption, including through the "Engel List" to target corrupt individuals through individual sanctions and revoking visas (Schneider, 2021). Although these efforts are sensible and broadly in line with the core thesis of this book, in all likelihood any attempt to address the "root causes" of migration will operate with a lag. This lagged effect has two implications: first, even if the policy is broadly correct, migration will remain a pressing challenge in the immediate term. Second, support for long-term strategies could be undermined by their seeming lack of near-term success. The challenge for the Biden Administration will be nurturing the public patience, political fortitude, and bipartisan backing necessary to see its sensible policies to completion; thus far, it is unclear whether the American electorate is willing to embrace a moderate, practical, and humanitarian approach to the Southwest border.

1.1 U.S. Strategic Interests in the Northern Triangle

The United States' policy toward the Northern Triangle has evolved since the first surge in migrants in the 2010s. At times, policy has leaned on local partners and inducements to address "root causes" of migration while exercising forbearance on border security policy, while other times U.S. policy veered toward emphasizing punitive measures to deter

[15] Despite these pledges, continued surges of border arrivals have overwhelmed the Department of Health and Human Services' Office of Refugee Resettlement. Courts have blocked the Biden Administration's efforts to end Trump's "Remain in Mexico" policy as well. See *The Economist* (2021).

inbound migration. Neither policy durably nor sufficiently changed on-the-ground realities, as migration continued throughout the Obama, Trump, and early Biden administrations. Rather than suggesting tactical changes to existing U.S. policy that would likely be overtaken by events, this book emphasizes first principles to ground guidance for U.S. policy toward the region.

There are three facets to U.S. strategy toward the Northern Triangle. First, since the founding of the United States, U.S. foreign policy has sought to achieve territorial security and economic advantages in the Western Hemisphere, first through westward expansion across the North American continent and then through pursuing an increasingly muscular policy vis-à-vis the domestic politics of other countries in the Western Hemisphere. The goal of regional preeminence is to preserve the United States' freedom of action in its immediate geographic neighborhood and, by extension, preventing hostile foreign powers from using the Western Hemisphere as a staging area to threaten the U.S. homeland.[16] The premise of this strategy is that geography matters, and thus regional preeminence can be a guarantor of security and relative stability. Maintaining a sphere of influence in the so-called U.S. "backyard" could help the United States promote governments with aligning interests and reduce the latitude of foreign powers to challenge U.S. influence and security, diplomatic, and economic interests in the Western Hemisphere (Mearsheimer, 2018, 222–223; Mearsheimer & Walt, 2016).[17] Second, the United States has a strategic interest in mitigating risks from potential regional spillovers from, inter-alia, drug trafficking, migration, and

[16] Importantly, U.S. Western Hemisphere hegemony, or at least U.S.-supported Western Hemisphere stability, also permits the United States to divert national resources to project power in other key strategic areas, including Europe, Northeast Asia, and the Persian Gulf. This luxury of power projection is unavailable to countries in more contested regions.

[17] Regarding U.S. security interests in Latin America, Ryan Berg and Hal Brands highlight how the United States has generally pursued a policy of *strategic denial* of other great powers in Latin America. They contend that this policy seeks to "prevent major rivals from developing regional footholds from which they can menace, distract, or otherwise undercut the strategic interests of the United States." The authors describe China's increasing involvement in Latin America as a contemporary challenge for the United States, particularly due to China's promotion of autocracy over democracy in places such as El Salvador, see Berg and Brands (2021).

other regional shocks. Again, these spillovers pose risks to the U.S. national interest by challenging existing government institutions' ability to contain the fallout from these shocks and increasing political tensions, in turn challenging the United States' political authority and domestic unity and reducing domestic consensus on key issues.[18] Third, the United States seeks to promote its democratic values and prosperity through free trade and pro-market policies. Although application of this principle has often been subordinated to more urgent political priorities (leading the United States to support, for instance, repressive governments perceived to preserve political order and eschew allegiances with foreign adversaries), the United States has generally pursued a policy of democracy and capitalism promotion in the region, particularly after the end of the Cold War. Although there are moral reasons for supporting representative government and economic freedom, there is also a realist logic that guides U.S. foreign policy: likeminded governments with similar institutions will be more inclined to support U.S. interests in the region, *ceteris paribus* (Dobson & Marsh, 2006, 185–188). Taken together, it follows from these strategic interests—preserving hegemony in the Western Hemisphere, reducing the potential for destabilizing adverse spillovers from and within the region, and promoting U.S. values—that the United States has a strong interest in preserving political order in the Northern Triangle and enhancing governance in the region. In light of these strategic interests, this chapter discusses principles of pursuing those interests in the Northern Triangle.[19]

[18] As argued by Robert Zoellick, U.S. foreign policy prioritized preserving domestic cohesion as a key goal which often biased the United States toward a more isolationist foreign policy, particularly in the nineteenth century. For more, see Zoellick (2020, 19–21). For President Dwight Eisenhower also saw the rise of the "military-industrial complex" as a risk to America's republican institutions and values, see Ambrose and Brinkley (1997, 169).

[19] There are also historical and cultural connections between the United States and Central America. Some of the drivers of these connections include the large Central American diaspora communities in the United States, cultural connections, the U.S. history in Panama (including the U.S. role in Panama's independence, and the U.S. construction of the Panama Canal), and the relatively high U.S. popularity in Central America, among other reasons.

1.2 *Recommended Principles of U.S. Engagement in the Northern Triangle*

Principle 1: Engage imperfect partners when interests coincide while managing the tradeoff between stability and democratic accountability.

A tension in U.S. foreign policy toward the Northern Triangle is the extent to which the United States prioritizes promoting accountable government with free and fair elections, human rights protections, strong democratic institutions, and supporting open societies, on one hand, while sponsoring regimes that are favorably disposed to the United States but might not share these U.S. values. During the Cold War, the United States often opted for stability over democratic accountability in the Northern Triangle. As mentioned previously, the United States supported a coup against a democratically elected government in Guatemala in the 1950s, while in the 1980s, the United States provided military assistance and training to El Salvador's government and military to maintain political cohesion during a brutal civil war in which nearly 75,000 Salvadorans died (Bonner, 2018; David, 1987, 34–35). One of the costs of this strategy is that prioritizing near-term stability often entrenches governments that are less sensitive to the needs of their broader populations and lack incentives to build more transparent institutions to enhance governance. State capacity lags, creating space for transnational criminal organizations (TCOs), corruption, and informality to thrive. This status quo bias in U.S. foreign policy can therefore be self-defeating in the long run. Still, unconditional U.S. support for democratization over other interests runs the risk of foregoing potential cooperation in areas where interests between the United States and an authoritarian or anti-democratic government align.[20]

[20] It also may conflate the means of achieving greater accountability, such as via democratization, with the end of more accountable government and enhanced governance. In some cases, greater democratization and public representation could create near-term governance vulnerabilities as newly elected governments may be tempted to use the state apparatus to settle scores and challenge the existing political, economic, and social orders of the country. Hence, support for democracy and open societies has often conflicted with near-term, realpolitik calculations of the national interest. This pattern is manifest in U.S. relations with, for example, several Arab authoritarian states today, post-War South Korea, the People's Republic of China since 1972, as well as Chile and Peru in Latin America, among many others. For more on illiberal democracies, see Zakaria (1997).

How should the United States navigate this tension? Policymakers should be pragmatic. They should recognize that international cooperation requires working with imperfect partners. But, when possible, policy should not lose sight of the promotion of U.S. values. Simply working with the United States should not inoculate partners from legitimate criticism about domestic repression, particularly when repression undermines governance and economic performance. Policy toward the Northern Triangle should thus be prepared to push back against the most egregious human rights violations and cases of corruption on both moral and realpolitik grounds. At other times, non-representative governments in the Northern Triangle will be willing to advance U.S. interests, for instance by undertaking economic reforms such as those outlined in the previous chapter. Pragmatism will require difficult tradeoffs and a recognition that democracy promotion and governance reform are mutually reinforcing in the long run but could face short-term tradeoffs. This balancing act will continue to be complicated by China's increasing engagement in Central America, especially when China is willing to look past (and implicitly support) authoritarian impulses in the region.[21] U.S. policymakers should recognize these tensions as the table stakes of engaging with the Northern Triangle in a new era of great power competition.

Principle 2: When possible, pursue multilateral action but do not rule out unilateral action if beneficial.

After World War II, the United States helped establish collective security arrangements and multilateral institutions, including the United Nations and the Bretton Woods institutions of the World Bank and International Monetary Fund, to maintain the liberal trade and monetary system (Brands, 2016). In the Western Hemisphere, the United States helped to found the OAS in 1948 to serve as a multilateral political forum to strengthen peace and security and to limit communist influence in the Western Hemisphere (Lee & Renwick, 2020). At the same time, when the United States' vital interests were threatened, often in Latin America but most recently in the Persian Gulf, the United States bypassed multilateral structures and pursued unilateral action (Dobson & Marsh, 2006).

[21] For a summary of President Nayib Bukele's embrace of China, see Linthicum (2022). As of end-January 2021, China pledged up to $500 million to El Salvador, including for projects such as water treatment plants, port infrastructure, a library, and a new stadium in San Salvador.

The choice between multilateralism and unilateralism is often a choice between international legitimacy and expediency. Voluntarily restraining U.S. behavior through a web of multilateral institutions creates space to reconcile disparate points of view among governments and, when actions are taken, frames them as representing the will of the international community. Moreover, multilateral coalitions are a source of political, economic, and diplomatic resources for the United States. Conversely, unilateralism has the benefit of not needing to coordinate through complex international institutions and ad-hoc political coalitions. That said, unilateral action risks reinforcing the perception that the United States retains an imperialistic attitude toward Latin America, reminiscent of the "Monroe Doctrine" era. Channeling American resources through multilateral institutions could dilute the impact of American action, especially when these resources need to be reconciled with foreign command, control, and coordination structures. Optimizing between the costs and benefits of multilateralism and unilateralism is challenging, and policymakers' first preference should be to explore whether partnerships with international institutions are feasible or issue-based multilateral coalitions can be formed to pursue shared goals prior to acting unilaterally. When multilateralism fails—or is impractical because of the complexity of coordination, difficulty of building consensus, or lack of interest among potential partner international institutions and governments—and vital United States interests are at stake, then unilateral action may be necessary.

Multilateral actions have a special role to play in addressing governance weakness in the Northern Triangle, including by creating and maintaining vertical anti-corruption accountability mechanisms. These mechanisms, such as the international corruption missions of the defunct International Commission against Corruption and Impunity in El Salvador (CICIES), International Commission Against Impunity in Guatemala (CICIG), and Mission in Support of the Fight against Corruption and Impunity in Honduras (MACCIH), can help improve governance in the Northern Triangle by rooting out corrupt actors and strengthening accountability. Although these multilateral anti-corruption commissions were imperfect, including relying on local partners for implementation for legitimacy at the potential expense of effectiveness, uneven funding, and perceptions of imperialism, their focus on improving institutional quality and eradicating corruption coincides with U.S. interests in the region. To the extent that these missions are viewed as arms-length from the United

States, they have an extra layer of embedded legitimacy by not simply being viewed as derivative of U.S. interests in the region, but instead aspiring to a higher ideal of good governance grounded in multilateral consensus. Multilateral vertical accountability mechanisms can also compensate for the lack of domestic governance capacity in the Northern Triangle countries. To rebuild these or similar institutions in the Northern Triangle, the United States should consider putting conditions on bilateral assistance and urging multilateral institutions to include participation in anti-impunity missions as conditions for grants and loans.

Although multilateralism can enhance the legitimacy of United States' actions in the Northern Triangle, there are some cases where unilateralism can help achieve the United States' interests. Unilateral actions can address governance weakness in the Northern Triangle by punishing actors that engage in illicit financial activity through the United States financial system and its affiliates. For instance, U.S. anti-money laundering (AML) enforcement actions can compensate for the lack of domestic AML enforcement in Northern Triangle countries, especially when the Northern Triangle's domestic institutions are underdeveloped and face capacity or political constraints. The same is true for the U.S. Department of Justice's demonstrated capacity to combat corruption and narcotics trafficking in the Northern Triangle. As an example, United States authorities arrested, tried, and convicted Tony Hernández, the brother of Honduras' President Juan Orlando Hernández, for drug trafficking (Anderson, 2021). Use of the Engel List, which includes the names of individuals in the Northern Triangle suspected of corruption, could be another useful unilateral measure, insofar as threats of losing visas, being placed on the U.S. Treasury's Office of Foreign Assets Control's Specially Designated Nationals and Blocked Persons List, and imposing sanctions under the Magnitsky Act alter individuals' cost–benefit analysis in engaging in corrupt activities (House Foreign Affairs Committee, 2020).

Finally, the United States should not limit its foreign policy toward the Northern Triangle to bilateral and regional engagement. Rather, multiple likeminded countries also face migration challenges, which could create space for cooperation, knowledge sharing, and joint initiatives to tackle the root causes of migration worldwide. For instance, the United States' treaty ally Germany faces migration challenges from the Middle East and Northern Africa, which impacts all of Europe. While Europe is preoccupied by events unfolding in its near abroad, the United States should emphasize the importance of commonalities in its policies toward the Northern Triangle vis-à-vis the challenges experienced in Europe. Elevating migration as a globally systemically important challenge, on par with other issues such as pandemics and climate change, could also help build an international consensus for addressing governance weakness in origin countries. Doing so could unlock funding and technical assistance from European partners, who could be induced to help the United States tackle migration challenges due to the impact of such challenges on U.S. domestic politics thus foreign policy.

Principle 3: Bring the Northern Triangle into the North American community.

Since the end of the Cold War, the United States has pursued a strategy of North American integration. As Robert Zoellick argues, the North American Free Trade Agreement (NAFTA) signed in 1992 was not just a trade deal designed to reduce tariffs in North America, although it did liberalize trade between Canada, Mexico, and the United States considerably. Rather, NAFTA reflected a deliberate strategy to draw Mexico into a broader society of North America, helping Mexico consolidate its new democracy, create space for civil society, and boost its economic growth. Further, by drawing Canada and Mexico closer to the United States, the United States enhanced its strategic depth by raising North America's income and American access to Mexico's resources, including hydrocarbons and Mexico's relatively young and less expensive workforce (Zoellick, 2020, 446). Although NAFTA has faced challenges, it has nevertheless had notable, on-the-ground successes, including the creation and deepening of North American value chains that increased competitiveness of companies in all three countries (Petraeus et al., 2014). It has continued to play that role since the negotiation of a successor agreement, the United States-Mexico-Canada Agreement (USCMA). Additionally, the renewed United States emphasis on supply chain resilience and near-shoring could serve as a tailwind for North and Central American integration, provided Mexico and the Northern Triangle countries continue to improve their business climates (Schott & Goodman, 2021).

Going forward, the United States should view the Northern Triangle countries as important to the North American project, as spillovers from the region have implications for Mexico's security and relations with the United States. Cooperation between Mexico and the Northern Triangle, bolstered by Canadian and American expertise, private capital, foreign aid, and political leadership, could enhance security and economic dynamism throughout the region.[22] Through diplomatic forums such as recently revived the North American Leaders' Summit, the United States could involve the Northern Triangle countries in multilateral policy planning discussions along a wide range of areas of mutual interest.[23] Such track 1 diplomacy could dovetail into track 1.5 and track 2 diplomacy, building bridges among civil society, the private sector, and governments in North America and the Northern Triangle (see principle 8). Doing so could help to create a shared sense of regional identity, which could facilitate cooperation on areas of mutual interest. Additionally, the United States and Mexico could explore broadening the mandate of the North American Development Bank, which has traditionally invested in border infrastructure between the United States and Mexico, to invest in regional border infrastructure in the Northern Triangle and provide technical assistance to the Northern Triangle governments.[24] For now, subpar infrastructure in the Northern Triangle limits the region's capacity to take full advantage of CAFTA-DR opportunities. To incentivize greater foreign investment and risk sharing, the United States can use sovereign bond guarantees to crowd in foreign investment in the Northern Triangle countries, including through novel structures such as green bonds.[25] Also, the United States could consider allowing the Northern Triangle countries to participate in North American regional financing arrangements, including through the United States' Exchange Stabilization Fund.[26] Such participation can enhance the Northern Triangle's fiscal and external sustainability while drawing the countries closer to the United States, Canada, and Mexico. Finally, the United States can push for greater cooperation and harmonization on trade, seeking to establish a North American free trade

[22] The United States can also encourage collaboration among Mexico and the Northern Triangle countries per *the Comprehensive Development Plan for El Salvador, Guatemala, Honduras, and south-southeast Mexico*, as argued in the subsequent section.

[23] For a summary of the 2021 North American Leaders Summit, including expert views and topics covered, see Wilson Center (2021). For a strong defense of the North American Leaders Summit process, see Jacobson and Wayne (2021). See Manak (2022) for a defense of continued North American integration after USMCA.

[24] For more on the North American Development Bank, see North American Development Bank (2021).

[25] See Morris et al. (2022) on the United States sovereign bond guarantee program.

[26] See Department of the Treasury (2021, 4) for more on the North America Framework Agreement. For a background on regional financing arrangements, see European Stability Mechanism (n.d.).

zone that encompasses the Northern Triangle. The United States should encourage the Northern Triangle countries to take advantage of existing trade deals such as CAFTA-DR—including through cumulation provisions on textiles with Mexico—while urging the establishment of regional value chains that include the Northern Triangle countries, including by addressing tariff and non-tariff barriers to trade.[27] Together, these actions could strengthen the Northern Triangle's integration into the North American community, allowing these countries to share in the prosperity and security provided by Hemispheric integration.[28]

Principle 4: Help the Northern Triangle navigate global threats such as pandemics and climate change.

The Northern Triangle countries are particularly vulnerable to global shocks, including pandemics and climate change. The United States has a strategic interest in helping the Northern Triangle countries navigate these shocks, lest they destabilize the Northern Triangle countries and lead to further migration flows. Potential forms of support to fight pandemics could include distributing tests, vaccines, therapeutics, and personal protective equipment; enhancing information sharing mechanisms among health ministries to track viral spread; supporting pandemic preparedness through capacity development of health ministries and the development of early warning systems; and strengthening macroeconomic resilience in the face of pandemics through mechanisms such as knowledge sharing, exchanges, and support for borrowing and grants at the individual-country level.

According to the Inter-American Dialogue and scholars from Berkeley University, the Northern Triangle is particularly vulnerable to climate

[27] Steve Liston argues that relaxing rules of origin requirements for CAFTA-DR countries, especially for the textiles and apparels industry. Liston claims that existing requirements are too strict, and loosening them to allow for some fabric to be sourced outside of the CAFTA-DR trading area would help develop regional value chains in textiles production; see Liston (2022). The National Council of Textile Organizations claims that the current "yarn forward" rules of origin provision create incentives to invest in North and Central American supply chains and that relaxing these rules of origin requirements would make the United States even more dependent on imports from China, and thus more exposed to global supply chain disruptions; see National Council of Textile Organizations (2022).

[28] Encouragingly, Mexico, which also suffers negative impacts from disorderly Central American migration, has shown increasing willingness to address the "root causes," including underdevelopment in neighboring economies. In 2018, for example, President Andrés Manuel López Obrador called for a "Marshall Plan" for the Northern Triangle.

change due to its poor infrastructure quality, latitude, and food insecurity, wherein extreme weather events disrupt the food supply chain, with downstream effects on employment and poverty. These researchers project that by 2050, climate-related shocks will cause an additional 3.9 million climate refugees to emigrate from the Northern Triangle (Inter-American Dialogue, 2021; Othering & Belonging Institute, n.d.). The Northern Triangle governments recognize the threat posed by climate change and have developed climate change strategies, yet all three countries have severe capacity constraints and funding limitations. It will be important for the United States to provide assistance to these countries to navigate the climate crisis, building on efforts such as the United States Agency for International Development work on climate change to improve their climate resilience over time, including through efforts to build adaptive capacity, mitigate greenhouse gas emissions by investing in low-carbon energy, and supporting a global carbon price to internalize climate risk.

Principle 5: Reaffirm the United States commitment to the liberal global trade and monetary order.

The United States helped to establish and maintain a liberal global trade and monetary order in the wake of World War II.[29] Currently, the rise of populism, polarization, and changing global power balances are straining this consensus-based system. Domestically, the United States has become ambivalent in continuing its historic willingness to underwrite the global trade and monetary order.[30] Gains from trade are not perceived to be equitably shared. Neoliberal economic institutions have come under strain due to successive global economic crises. The rise of China, resurgence of Russia, and political fissures in Europe increased global discord on key issues related to the rules-based multilateral trading

[29] For a foundational text on *hegemonic stability theory*, including the role the hegemon plays in maintaining the global political economy, see Kindleberger (1986). Kindleberger argues that global economic stability follows from the actions of a leading state willing to bear the costs of maintaining the international economic system, including by serving as a consumer and lender of last resort, stabilizing exchange rates, and helping to steer global macroeconomic policy coordination.

[30] G. John Ikenberry provides a good summary of the challenges facing liberal internationalism, see Ikenberry (2020). Haass (2021) describes the limitations of America First foreign policy, while Kupchan (2020) explains the logics of neo-isolationism in the United States today.

system, sovereign debt, global macroeconomic imbalances, capital flows, among issues.

While the United States has legitimate concerns about the excesses of this system and fair claims about the need for burden-sharing in the maintenance and adjustment within this system, a haphazard withdrawal from the liberal global trade and monetary order is not in the United States' interests. Rather, withdrawal will exacerbate many of the inequities and issues plaguing the United States today, from perceptions of economic precarity and inflation, to concerns about migration. Thus, the United States has a strategic interest in the maintenance of the liberal global trade and monetary system from which the Northern Triangle countries directly benefit. Supporting this system should be viewed as an anchor of U.S. engagement in the Northern Triangle, recognizing that the alternative of U.S. withdrawal and a more entropic global political economy would undermine U.S. interests globally.

Principle 6: Designate bureaucratic champions while adopting a whole-of-government approach to engagement.

One of the challenges of achieving policy coherence in the Northern Triangle is coordinating actions across multiple agencies of government, all with their own interests and priorities. In theory, the National Security Council of the White House should play that role. In reality, the National Security Council-led interagency process can be chaotic, with government agencies vying for influence or trying to protect their bureaucratic turf from perceived White House overreach.[31] Some of this tension is unavoidable—after all, striking the right balance of bottom-up, agency-led initiatives within a top-down strategy articulated by the president always will be messy. At the same time, promoting U.S. policy coherence may require the designation of a high-ranking administration official, such as the vice president, national security advisor, or secretaries of state or treasury, or even the attorney general (given this book's focus on governance) to serve as the administration's point person on all issues related

[31] Robert Gates, secretary of defense during the Barack Obama Administration, documented the challenges of navigating interagency processes in his 2015 memoir, see Gates (2014, 352). John Bolton, President Donald Trump's national security advisor, also critiques interagency process, particularly when cabinet officials attempted to defend their turf from what they saw as White House meddling, see Bolton (2020).

to the Northern Triangle.[32] As framed by Petraeus et al., such a "champion" can provide "continuous" rather than "episodic" attention to the Northern Triangle (Petraeus et al., 2014, 63). Administrations may find it difficult to identify a high-ranking official willing to take on such a challenging portfolio, so it will be important to balance the assignment of the Northern Triangle, which can be viewed as a high risk, low reward assignment, with other portfolios that are more likely to yield political dividends. The president can emphasize that the Northern Triangle remains a core strategic area of focus for the United States, on par with Western Europe, Northeast Asia, and the Persian Gulf. Such an elevation of the issue could help make the Northern Triangle seem like an attractive portfolio and possible springboard to greater responsibilities. Finally, the champion should seek to build strong links to the legislative branch and other key stakeholders to assure broad and bipartisan support (see next principle).

Principle 7: Build a bipartisan consensus for action on governance in the Northern Triangle.

The United States Congress is a key stakeholder in the formulation of U.S. foreign policy. While the executive branch sets the agenda and represents the U.S. government in diplomatic engagements, the Congress has the "power of the purse" and the jurisdiction to declare war, pass treaties, and veto executive branch foreign policy appointments (Leyton-Brown, 1982). As a result, the legislative and executive branches share powers in foreign policy development. Amicable relations between the executive and legislature, particularly during periods of divided government where the legislature has political incentives to thwart executive branch initiatives, enhances the U.S. strategic depth by ensuring that foreign policy does not become yet another partisan battlefield. Congressional buy-in also contributes to foreign policy consistency and policy coherence. As Robert Zoellick notes, foreign policy often requires balancing long-term foreign strategic interests with near-term domestic political needs; that is particularly true for U.S. Latin America policy, given the influence of diaspora communities, economic and security interdependence, and border considerations. Often, the latter constrains the former, so skilled negotiators work both angles to develop a congressional constituency and interest

[32] The Biden administration has adopted this approach by assigning the vice president the Central America portfolio and designating a state department Northern Triangle special envoy.

group support for long-term foreign policy priorities (Zoellick, 2020, 455–457). In other cases, when the executive and legislative branches disagree, the lack of domestic political consensus could neuter foreign policy decision-making. Foreign interlocutors, knowing that a president does not have congressional backing or expecting the opposition to retake the White House in the near term and adopt different policy priorities, may be less inclined to make concessions to the United States during negotiations.[33]

In the case of the Northern Triangle, the executive branch will need to prioritize building a domestic political consensus for action. Tactically, it may be prudent to divorce discussions of immigration policy reform from U.S. strategy in Central America until the political temperature on immigration dissipates. Despite the polarization in Congress, there are signs that helping the Northern Triangle countries enjoys bipartisan support in Congress, as evidenced by broad bipartisan support of the United States-Northern Triangle Enhanced Engagement Act in December 2020 (Runde, 2021). Moreover, executive branch officials should contextualize U.S. support for the Northern Triangle within the broader strategic imperatives of U.S. interests in the Western Hemisphere, including related to preserving United States' influence in its near abroad and countering the rising influence of China in the region, and not just as a means to contain adverse spillovers from outbound migration. Doing so can ensure that bipartisan support for governance assistance to the Northern Triangle remains constant over time and is linked to other areas of bipartisan consensus, including issues related to China. Strong Congressional outreach, briefings, and joint study trips to the Northern Triangle countries can further build a bipartisan culture of assisting the Northern Triangle countries.

Principle 8: Engage the private sector and civil society.

Lasting change in the Northern Triangle will require an alliance between the U.S. private sector, civil society and government, and their

[33] Of course, there are downsides to too much consensus. As argued by Stephen Walt, groupthink among the legislative and executive branches can cause foreign policy makers to become "wedded to a bunch of bad ideas and to a flawed grand strategy, the result [of which] is likely to be a protracted series of failures" (Walt, 2019). Thus, a more activist Congress can reign in the excesses of executive power, as occurred during the 1970s after the Vietnam War. For more, see Leyton-Brown (1982), Lindsay (1992), and Zoellick (1999).

counterparts in the Northern Triangle. The Northern Triangle countries have large diasporas in the United States that, if engaged, could be a catalyst for future reforms. The United States should view diaspora members as potential civil society and private sector leaders in the U.S.–Northern Triangle relationship and invest in these relationships through initiatives such as the 100,000 Strong in the Americas, which provides grants to strengthen educational exchanges between the United States and the Western Hemisphere. Additionally, leveraging the private sector through targeted tax relief and other inducements to invest in the Northern Triangle countries could help the Northern Triangle countries increase potential growth and address structural bottlenecks that perpetuate governance trap conditions over time. Finally, public and private sector cooperation through mechanisms such as credit enhancements and loan guarantees, political risk insurance, and technical assistance can "crowd in" American investment in the Northern Triangle, including programs provided by the Development Finance Corporation (U.S. International Development Finance Corporation, n.d.).[34]

Principle 9: Distinguish between acute and chronic challenges in the Northern Triangle. Accept that governance reform, while a long-term solution to the region's challenges, may not deliver immediate results.

The previous chapter highlighted a number of reforms that the Northern Triangle countries could pursue that, if implemented fully, have the potential to help these countries escape their governance traps. But escaping the governance trap is rarely a linear or fast process—rather, reform efforts often proceed in a stop–start manner, subject to the political rhythms in the United States and the Northern Triangle and shaped by the preferences of political and economic elites, with frequent roll-backs of hard-won gains. U.S. officials should recognize that governance vulnerabilities are one of the "root causes" of outbound migration but that addressing these vulnerabilities, while necessary, will not happen overnight. Rather, improving governance is a generational project that involves deep structural, cultural, political, and economic reforms change

[34] Some critics of the Biden administration's "root causes" strategy believe that it could risk over-prioritizing U.S. engagement with civil society actors at the expense of the government. Finding the right balance between engaging the various levels of the Northern Triangle societies will be difficult, but since potential reformers can be found in multiple places, the United States should cast a wide net for potential support.

in these countries. While addressing chronic governance weaknesses can yield dividends, the Northern Triangle is likely to produce acute flare-ups that cannot be addressed exclusively with long-term reforms. A practical foreign policy should thus seek to optimize between short-term palliatives (e.g., humanitarian assistance after key shocks) and long-term initiatives (i.e., institution building and enhancing accountability and governance) to pursue U.S. interests and, critically, differentiate the two time horizons when crafting policy. U.S. leaders will need to manage domestic public expectations to communicate that governance reform can address chronic problems in the region, but is not a panacea.

Principle 10: Prepare for breakthroughs but be realistic about the frequency of windows of opportunity for reform.

The American diplomat Philip Gordon wrote that "the bias of American political culture, resulting from the country's record of achievement and belief in its own exceptionalism, is to believe every problem has a solution, and the bias of the U.S. government is to act forcefully to try to solve those problems, no matter how difficult they might appear" (Gordon, 2020, 276). While Gordon was talking about U.S. foreign policy toward the Middle East, his caveat could apply to policymakers working on the Northern Triangle. No matter America's best efforts, entropic forces can win out, and sometimes, America's best response is to refrain from intervening too heavily in the domestic affairs of other countries, as doing so is often subject to unintended consequences that may ultimately exacerbate the problem policymakers are trying to solve. There will be times when the Northern Triangle's governments will be impervious to U.S. influence, while other times, such as during national crises or after elections, a window of opportunity for sweeping reforms could open. It will be important for the United States to have a robust set of potential reforms, with appropriate inducements, "on the shelf" and ready to be implemented when conditions are right. However, the default condition for the Northern Triangle will likely be one where the openness to foreign influence on reforms is low, and therefore U.S. policy should seek incremental change on a narrower set of priorities. In short, the United States should be prepared for breakthroughs when sweeping reforms can take place but be realistic that status quo bias and stickiness of governance traps will make such reform agendas difficult during most periods.

2 Canada and Mexico

It is not obvious that Canada has strategic interests in the Northern Triangle. After all, Canada enjoys geographic isolation from Central America, with the United States and Mexico bearing the brunt of outbound migration from the region. Nevertheless, Canada does have strategic interests in the Northern Triangle that extend beyond humanitarian considerations such as fulfilling Canada's historic role as a refuge for immigrants (Cheatham, 2020; Pison, 2019). This strategic interest stems from Canada's reliance on the United States as an economic and security partner in the Western Hemisphere. The Northern Triangle matters to Canada because adverse spillovers from the region can have knock-on effects for its relations with the United States. A more entropic Northern Triangle runs the risk of inflaming U.S. internal political divisions related to border security and immigration policy, as was evident in the election and subsequent presidency of Donald Trump. As a presidential candidate, Trump railed against border insecurity and repeatedly questioned the wisdom of international trade accords, including the North American Free Trade Agreement (NAFTA). To the extent that these two strands of thought—strengthening border security and embracing protectionism—represent a coherent governing paradigm for the United States, it stands to reason that heightened tensions in one area such as border security may decrease the appeal of closer collaboration with America's neighbors. After all, while in office Trump did not hesitate to threaten trade sanctions and outright abrogation of NAFTA unless Mexico and Canada agreed to concessions related to border security cooperation, rules of origin requirements, and liberalizing agriculture trade, among others. While the NAFTA renegotiation ultimately resolved in Canada and Mexico's favor with the effectiveness of USMCA as NAFTA's successor in 2020, this episode highlights that the United States' commitment to liberal trading relationships with North America is not guaranteed, and thus the potential rollback of the United States' embrace of the North American project is likely viewed as an existential threat in Ottawa.

According to political scientists Charles Doran and David Pratt, Canada can play a key role anchoring a global association of leading democracies, helping to preserve the international political order amid changing power balances and foreign policy roles of the leading states in the international system. In such a context, "working closely with the United States will be especially critical" (Doran & Pratt, 2012). Canada should view the Northern Triangle as a strategic opportunity to show value to the United States while hedging against criticisms from a future U.S. leader who might share Trump's skepticism about the value of U.S. diplomatic relationships. Areas of collaboration could include deepening trade and investment links with the Northern Triangle, including by signing onto bilateral commercial initiatives between the United States and the Northern Triangle countries and potentially charting a path for the Northern Triangle countries to join the USMCA or, at a minimum, allow Mexico to source goods from the Northern Triangle countries covered by the United States-Dominican Republic-Central America (CAFTA-DR) and retain duty-free access under the USMCA (Rooney, 2021). Additionally, Canada should admit more asylum seekers from Central America, in line with its historic responsiveness to refugee crises, including in Syria in the 2010s. That would decrease political pressure in the United States and diminish the impetus toward some of the United States' more extreme policies (Llana, 2019).[35] Finally, as a consummate "middle power," Canada directs its efforts toward building coalitions of likeminded states and by promoting multilateral cooperation and restraint. As argued by John Ravenhill, it is Canada's relative weakness compared to leading states such as the United States, China, and Russia that gives it credibility to help craft diplomatic solutions to international challenges (Ravenhill, 1998). In Latin America, Canada's lack of historical baggage compared to the United States gives it a particularly important potential role as a mediator and policy tutor. Thus, Canada could serve as an honest broker in pushing cooperation between the United States, Mexico, and the Northern Triangle countries. Already, Canada is playing that role in the Lima Group, an ad hoc organization established to address the crisis in Venezuela. Ottawa should show similar leadership in Central America.

Mexico has distinct interests in Central America. Mexico has its own problems related to organized crime and the rule of law and lacks the resources to confront these challenges domestically, let alone address similar challenges in the Northern Triangle. Nevertheless, Mexico has strategic interests in the Northern Triangle, which include ensuring that

[35] Former Canadian Prime Minister Joe Clark noted how Canada's policies toward the Northern Triangle and Central America broadly differed historically from the United States' heavy-handed approach, including by promoting human rights, democracy, and admitting refugees. For more, see Clark (2014).

developments in the Northern Triangle do not undermine the United States–Mexico relationship, leveraging Central American labor to increase economic growth in Southern Mexico, and addressing migration through Mexico. Like Canada, Mexico has an interest in ensuring that political blowback in the United States related to migration does not undermine its bilateral relationship with its northern neighbor. Mexico's challenge is to preserve amicable relations with the United States while not overpromising on its ability to address the "root causes" of migration in the Northern Triangle. To do so, Mexico should be prepared to take a North American approach to Central America, harmonizing trade and investment policies between North America and the Northern Triangle in an attempt to pull the Northern Triangle countries into Mexico's regional sphere of influence.[36] Recently, Mexico prioritized multilateral initiatives in the Northern Triangle, helping to develop the *Comprehensive Development Plan for El Salvador, Guatemala, Honduras, and south-southeast Mexico* in conjunction with the United Nations Economic Commission for Latin America and the Caribbean (ECLAC), released in September 2021. This plan covers Mexico's nine southernmost states as well as the Northern Triangle and rests on four pillars: economic development, environmental sustainability, social well-being, and management of the migration cycle. The plan includes proposals for 114 projects worth about $45 billion over five years covering areas such as biodiversity, strengthening monetary policy transmission, and energy (United Nations, 2021). While it is too soon to tell how effective the *Comprehensive Development Plan* will be, and who will pay for it, it nevertheless signals that Mexico views the Northern Triangle countries as key partners in developing Southern Mexico, which historically lags the North and other industrial hubs in Mexico in terms of per-capita income, growth, and productivity. Mexico should consider engaging the United States on these efforts, including by securing technical assistance and funding, through novel financing structures and risk sharing with the private sector. Mexico and the United States have already agreed to extensive security cooperation and an increase in Mexico's asylum capacity and to cooperate on development assistance between USAID and its Mexican counterpart, the Mexican Agency for International Cooperation and Development (AMEXCID) (U.S. Department of State, 2021).

[36] Doing so would also allow Mexico to serve as a regional counterweight to Brazil, as argued by Rafael Fernández de Castro, see Fernández de Castro (2015).

Finally, it will be important for Mexico to continue to allay historic fears that greater integration with the United States comes at the expense of closer relations with Central America—a common concern of Northern Triangle countries (Jaubert et al., 2019). Just as Canada could be a more effective envoy to the Northern Triangle than the United States, the same is true for Mexico, which brings cultural and linguistic commonalities and geographic proximity to its interactions with the Northern Triangle governments and other actors.

3 International Partners

There are several other key players who will help shape the prospects for reform in the Northern Triangle countries. They include the diasporas of Guatemala, Honduras, and El Salvador, civil society and private sector leaders, and international institutions.

All three of the Northern Triangle countries are heavily dependent on their diasporas. Nearly 10% of Northern Triangle nationals live in the United States. Remittances account for between 15 and 25% of gross domestic product and are the primary source of foreign exchange for the Northern Triangle countries. Simply put, the region's most productive export is its people. A key goal for the Northern Triangle countries should be to leverage their diaspora networks to foster inclusive growth and development. The links between diasporas and their origin countries extend beyond direct transfers. Jean-Baptiste Meyer argues that origin countries benefit from the human capital accumulation of their diasporas. Conducting a network analysis of diaspora communities, Meyer found that rather than signaling a "brain drain" from the origin countries, the diasporas contributed to a "brain gain" by facilitating knowledge development and diffusion. These sociotechnical and technoeconomic networks link different parts of the host country (e.g., the United States) with institutions in the origin countries (e.g., the Northern Triangle) (Meyer, 2008). Engaging the diaspora will be critical to helping the Northern Triangle countries escape their governance traps. Donors and partners should view the diaspora as a key stakeholder in the development of the Northern Triangle, investing in human capital development and skills transfer. The Northern Triangle countries should also investigate novel financing structures to tap the economic potential of their diasporas, including via diaspora bonds. As argued by Anupam Chandler, diaspora bonds, or a financing instrument by which issuers in origin countries (such as sovereigns, banks, households, and firms) borrow from diasporas, could be a viable mechanism of intermediating flows from the diaspora into productive investments. Diaspora bonds have the added benefit of potentially being governed by the securities laws of the home country to the benefit of the recipient country (Chandler, 2001). Partners and the Northern Triangle countries should also view their diasporas as cultural ambassadors from their countries. For instance, one study found that in the 1990s, Irish Americans proved helpful in lobbying the United States government for progress in the Northern Ireland peace process (Boyle & Kitchin, 2014).[37]

Civil society and the private sector are also critical stakeholders in the Northern Triangle that could help the Northern Triangle escape their governance traps. What are the benefits of a robust civil society in the context of governance reform? Friedman et al. argue that "a well-developed civil society aggregates and expresses the wishes of the public through a wealth of nongovernmental forms of association and safeguards public freedom by limiting the government's ability to impose arbitrary rule by force" (Friedman et al., 2001). Civil society can thus be a key counterweight to creeping authoritarianism, particularly in weak states with underdeveloped democratic institutions. Civil society, including independent journalists, can also serve as a check against corruption, highlighting abuses and holding potentially corrupt actors accountable in the court of public opinion. Regarding economic activity, strong civil society participation can help identify and serve as a voice for groups that could suffer short-term consequences from economic reforms, ensuring that these groups receive just consideration from political processes to protect against the reversal of reforms over time. In this sense, civil society engagement can preserve reforms when government dynamics shift. External stakeholders should seek to ensure that civil society inputs are considered when crafting policy toward the governments of the Northern Triangle. Cross-country connections among likeminded civil society groups could strengthen their cohesion and resource base, further preserving government accountability (Scholte, 2004).

The private sectors in the United States, Mexico, and the Northern Triangle are considerable stakeholders in helping the Northern Triangle countries escape their governance traps. Chronic governance weakness

[37] Segments of these diasporas are undocumented, and so their capacity to support U.S. policy in the Northern Triangle is curtailed.

reduces the return on investment for firms and households, in turn sapping economic growth and job creation. The region's governments should engage in policy dialogues with the private sector to ensure that private sector stakeholders' views are articulated during the policymaking process, while avoiding regulatory capture and corruption. These consultations can yield key insights about the regulatory barriers to greater private sector investment, infrastructure and human capital needs for firms, and high growth potential industries in which the Northern Triangle countries could specialize. Greater foreign direct investment (FDI) flows could facilitate knowledge and skills transfer to the broader population, multiplying the benefits of investment across the economy.[38] Additionally, the private sector could serve as a source of capital for the governments of the Northern Triangle. As discussed in the previous chapter, tapping foreign capital bases can be especially helpful in smoothing consumption for governments, firms, and households. Foreign partners can facilitate robust private sector involvement via FDI and portfolio flows through dialogues, credit enhancements, and other targeted incentives.[39]

The international financial institutions (IFIs), including the Inter-American Development Bank, World Bank, and the International Monetary Fund all engage in the Northern Triangle. All three institutions offer unique areas of expertise that could benefit the Northern Triangle countries. Yet their engagement should not be viewed as a silver bullet to achieve lasting development in the region. Additional loans and grants from the IFIs alone would not change the governance trap equilibria. Rather, financial and technical assistance could create the space for lasting reform conditional on strong national ownership of the reform agenda.

[38] Admittedly, the empirical link between FDI flows and growth is unclear and potentially endogenous (i.e., higher levels of GDP may contribute to FDI flows and vice versa, see Mavrotas and Chowdhury [2006]). Other authors identify a clear link between FDI flows and productivity growth, especially in capital-intensive sectors, see Cipollina et al. (2012). Even if the causal links between FDI and growth are muddied, it is logical to assume that a country's ability to attract FDI bodes well for its growth prospects.

[39] The United States in particular could have a comparative advantage in promoting private sector-led growth in the Northern Triangle by providing an alternative to state-led development paradigms, noting that its firms are held to high standards related to transparency and regular disclosures, which in turn provide a safeguard against misuse of funds and governance-related vulnerabilities. The United States' deep capital base could also be leveraged to help meet the development needs of the Northern Triangle.

Much like the United States, the IFIs must "pick their spots" and act when momentum is on their side, recognizing that engagement will likely continue in a stop–start pattern. Several principles should guide IFI engagement with the Northern Triangle. First, the institutions will have to navigate an increasingly polarized and competitive geopolitical landscape. These global dynamics could lead to institutional drift if the IFIs do not make best efforts to evolve with the times, including by finding common ground among their shareholders (G20 Eminent Persons Group, 2018). In the Northern Triangle, the IFIs can serve as arbiters of competition in several areas, including advising on appropriate development paradigms (i.e., market-oriented vs. statist), pushing for even-handed global debt standards related to debt transparency and debt vulnerabilities, and in helping the Northern Triangle countries make dispassionate assessments about specific projects (including from bilateral, non-Paris Club lenders), among other roles.[40] The IFIs should also seek to *complement* and *coordinate* their activities to maximize their impact and reduce duplication. Complementarity requires specializing within their respective areas of expertise, while coordinating can help the IFIs avoid race-to-the-bottom lending dynamics and promote information sharing and lessons learned. Deciding which IFI or bilateral should lead coordination can be difficult given turf battles and legitimate disagreements regarding the optimal approach in a given country. The host country should be given a say in the development process and empower a specific actor to help lead in coordination. Coordination should also span multiple countries, so regional perspectives and lessons learned can be disseminated across donors working on similar challenges.

4 Conclusion

The purpose of this chapter is to discuss how international partners could help the Northern Triangle countries escape their governance traps. Parties discussed include the United States, Canada, Mexico, civil society,

[40] Regarding different development paradigms between East and West, see Halper (2010). For a critique on the sustainability of the "Beijing Consensus," see Yao (2010). On state-led development in Latin America, see Smith (2018) and Orihuela (2019). On potential reforms of the international debt architecture, see Georgieva et al. (2020). Regarding the IMF's role in sovereign debt restructurings, see Hagan (2020). On the engagement of non-Paris Club creditors, including in the COVID-19 debt landscape, see Rieffel (2021).

the private sector, and the international financial institutions. This list of stakeholders is not exhaustive, and the landscape of political and economic engagement is changing. Still, from a historical perspective, the above actors had strong interests in the Northern Triangle and exercised considerable influence over the Northern Triangle's economic and political development. While these international partners could help the Northern Triangle countries escape their governance traps, international support cannot compensate for a lack of political will for reform within the countries. Sometimes, the right engagement strategy will be not to engage directly with the governments in question. Other times, when the moment is right, the international community should be willing to "strike while the iron is hot" when a reform-minded government comes through.[41] In either case, reforms are more likely to succeed when the host government exhibits strong ownership over reforms, has popular public backing or electoral leeway to undertake difficult reforms, and where international political will and attention can be sustained.

References

Alvarez, P. (2021, October 29). *Families forcibly separated at the border by the Trump administration seeking settlements in ongoing negotiations*. CNN.com. Retrieved December 1, 2021, from https://www.cnn.com/2021/10/29/politics/family-separation/index.html

Ambrose, S. E., & Brinkley, D. G. (1997). *Rise to globalism: American foreign policy since 1938* (8th ed.). Penguin Group.

American Immigration Council. (2021). *A guide to title 42 expulsions at the border* (Policy brief). American Immigration Council.

Anderson, J. L. (2021, November 8). Is the president of Honduras a narco-trafficker? *The New Yorker*. Retrieved January 25, 2022, from https://www.newyorker.com/magazine/2021/11/15/is-the-president-of-honduras-a-narco-trafficker

Beck, E. R. (2007). The good neighbor policy, 1933–1938. *The Historian, 2*, 110–131.

Berg, R. C., & Brands, H. (2021). *The return of geopolitics: Latin America and the Caribbean in an era of strategic competition* (Policy brief). Center for Strategic and International Studies.

[41] Said another way, windows of opportunity for reform will likely be open during critical junctures, and the international community should be ready to mobilize and tailor off-the-shelf support on a shortened timeline.

Bolton, J. (2020). *The room where it happened: A White House memoir*. Simon & Schuster.
Bonner, R. (2018, January 20). America's role in El Salvador's deterioration. *The Atlantic*. Retrieved December 1, 2021, from https://www.theatlantic.com/international/archive/2018/01/trump-and-el-salvador/550955/
Boyle, M., & Kitchin, R. (2014). Diaspora-centred development: Current practice, critical commentaries, and research priorities. In S. Sahoo & B. K. Pattanaik (Eds.), *Global diasporas and development: Socioeconomic, cultura, and policy perspectives* (pp. 17–39). Springer.
Brands, H. (2016). *American grand strategy and the liberal order: Continuity, Chagne, and options for the future*. Building a Sustainable International Order: A RAND Project to Explore U.S. Strategy in a Changing World. RAND Corporation.
Chandler, A. (2001). Diaspora bonds. *New York University Law Review, 76*(4), 1005–1099.
Cheatham, A. (2020, August 3). *What is Canada's immigration policy?* Council on Foreign Relations. Retrieved December 3, 2021, from https://www.cfr.org/backgrounder/what-canadas-immigration-policy
Cheatham, A. (2021, December 2). *U.S. detention of child migrants*. Council on Foreign Relations. Retrieved December 4, 2021, from https://www.cfr.org/backgrounder/us-detention-child-migrants
Cipollina, M., Giovannetti, G., Pietrovito, F., & Pozzolo, A. F. (2012). FDI and growth: What cross-country industry data say. *The World Economy, 35*(11), 1599–1629.
Clark, J. (2014). *How we lead: Canada in a century of change*. Penguin Random House Canada.
Congressional Research Service. (2018). *The Trump administration's "zero tolerance" immigration enforcement policy* (CRS Report). Congressional Research Service.
David, S. R. (1987). *Third World coups d'etat and International security*. Johns Hopkins University Press.
Department of the Treasury. (2021). *Audit of the exchange stabilization fund's financial statements for fiscal years 2020 and 2019* (Inspector General Report). Office of Inspector General.
Dobson, A. P., & Marsh, S. (2006). *US foreign policy since 1945* (2nd ed.). Routledge.
Doran, C. F., & Pratt, D. (2012). The need for a Canadian grand strategy. In *Canada's national security in the post-9/11 world: Strategy, interests, and threats* (pp. 25–44). University of Toronto Press.
Ellis, R. E. (2020). *China's advance in the Caribbean* (Policy brief). Wilson Center Latin American Program.

Ernst, J., Josh, K., Olson, E. L., Sample, K., & Zúñiga, R. (n.d.). *US foreign aid to the Northern Triangle 2014–2019: Promoting success by learning from the past.* Wilson Center.

European Stability Mechanism. (n.d.). *Regional Financing Arrangements (RFAs).* ESM. Retrieved January 25, 2022, from https://www.esm.europa.eu/about-us/how-we-work/regional-financing-arrangements-rfa#:~:text=Regional%20Financing%20Arrangements%20(RFAs)%20are,financial%20difficulties%20in%20their%20regions

Felter, C., & Cheatham, A. (2019). *Can 'safe third country' agreements resolve the asylum crisis?* (Brief). Council on Foreign Relations.

Fernández de Castro, R. (2015, February 3). Mexico's foreign policy agenda in Central America. *Americas Quarterly.* Retrieved December 1, 2021, from https://www.as-coa.org/articles/mexicos-foreign-policy-agenda-central-america

Friedman, E. J., Hochstetler, K., & Clark, A. M. (2001). Sovereign limits and regional opportunities for global civil society in Latin America. *Latin American Research Review, 36*(3), 7–35.

G20 Eminent Persons Group. (2018). *Making the global financial system work for all: Report of the G20 eminent persons group on global financial governance* (G20 Report). G20.

Gates, R. M. (2014). *Duty: Memoires of a secretary at war.* Vintage Books.

Georgieva, K., Pazarbasioglu, C., & Weeks-Brown, R. (2020, October 1). *Reform of the international debt architecture is urgently needed.* Imf.org. Retrieved December 10, 2020, from https://blogs.imf.org/2020/10/01/reform-of-the-international-debt-architecture-is-urgently-needed/

Gordon, P. H. (2020). *Losing the long game: The false promise of regime change in the Middle East.* St. Martin's Press.

Haass, R. (2021). The age of America first: Washington's flawed new foreign policy consensus. *Foreign Affairs, 100*(6).

Hagan, S. (2020). Sovereign debt restructuring: The centrality of the IMF's role. *SSRN Electronic Journal, 20*(13), 1–14.

Halper, S. (2010). *The Beijing consensus: How China's authoritarian model will dominate the twenty-first century.* Basic Books.

House Foreign Affairs Committee. (2020, December 22). *Engel U.S.-Northern Triangle Enhanced Engagement Act Passes Congress: Legislation requires creation of "Engel list" of corrupt and undemocratic actors who will be denied entry to U.S.* House Foreign Affairs Committee. Retrieved January 25, 2022, from https://foreignaffairs.house.gov/2020/12/engel-u-s-northern-triangle-enhanced-engagement-act-passes-congress

Ibe, P. (2020). *The dangers of Trump's "safe third country" agreements in Central America* (News and Commentary). American Freinds Service Committee.

Iesue, L. (2016, August 1). *The Alliance for prosperity plan: A failed effort for stemming migration*. Council on Hemispheric Affairs. Retrieved October 6, 2021, from https://www.coha.org/the-alliance-for-prosperity-plan-a-failed-effort-for-stemming-migration/

Ikenberry, G. J. (2020). *A world safe for democracy: Liberal internationalism and the crises of global order*. Yale University Press.

Imison, P. (2016, March 21). *Mexico's efforts to tackle police corruption keep failing*. Vice News. Retrieved October 5, 2020, from https://www.vice.com/en/article/j59a8x/mexicos-efforts-to-tackle-police-corruption-are-failing

Inter-American Dialogue. (2021). *Climate change in the Northern Triangle: Recommendations for US assistance* (Policy Brief). Inter-American Dialogue.

Jacobson, D., & Wayne, E. A. (2021, November 16). Resuming North American leaders summits could accomplish much. *The Globe and Mail*. Retrieved January 26, 2022, from https://www.theglobeandmail.com/business/commentary/article-resuming-north-american-leaders-summits-could-accomplish-much/

Jaubert, H. R., Castaneda, G., Hernandez, J., & Vuskovic, P. (2019). *The difficult triangle: Mexico, Central America, and the United States*. Routledge.

Kaplan, S. B. (2021). *Globalizing patient capital: The political economy of Chinese finance in the Americas*. Cambridge University Press.

Kindleberger, C. P. (1986). *The world in depression: 1929–1939*. University of California Press.

Kissinger, H. (1994). *Diplomacy*. Simon & Schuster.

Kupchan, C. A. (2020). *Isolationism: A history of America's efforts to shield itself from the world*. Oxford University Press.

Lee, B., & Renwick, D. (2020, March 10). *The organization of American states*. Council on Foreign Relations. Retrieved December 1, 2021, from https://www.cfr.org/backgrounder/organization-american-states

LeoGrande, W. M. (1990). From Reagan to Bush: The transition in US policy towards Central America. *Journal of Latin American Studies, 22*(3), 595–621.

LeoGrande, W. M. (1998). *Our own backyard: The United States in Central America, 1977–1992*. University of North Carolina Press.

Leyton-Brown, D. (1982). The role of congress in the making of foreign policy. *International Journal, 38*(1), 59–76.

Lindsay, J. M. (1992). Congress and foreign policy: Why the hill matters. *Political Science Quarterly, 107*(4), 607–628.

Linthicum, K. (2022, February 17). In Latin America's new Cold War, will China lift up autocrats? *Los Angeles Times*. Retrieved February 23, 2022, from https://www.latimes.com/world-nation/story/2022-02-17/as-china-encroaches-on-latin-america-what-happens-to-democracies

Liston, S. (2022, January 23). To stabilize Central America, the US must craft better incentives for trade. *The Hill*. Retrieved January 26, 2022, from https://thehill.com/opinion/finance/590727-to-stabilize-central-america-the-us-must-craft-better-incentives-for-trade

Llana, S. M. (2019, September 5). Canada asks, 'Why aren't we helping more Central American refugees?'. *The Christian Science Monitor*. Retrieved December 1, 2021, from https://www.csmonitor.com/World/Americas/2019/0905/Canada-asks-Why-aren-t-we-helping-more-Central-American-refugees

Lopez, O. (2021, January 14). Mexico exonerates ex-defense chief who was freed by the U.S. *The New York Times*. Retrieved February 8, 2022, from https://www.nytimes.com/2021/01/15/world/americas/mexico-defense-minister-cienfuegos.html

Manak, I. (2022). *North America, interrupted: Trade, politics, and a stunted continental vision* (Working Paper). Wilson Center.

Mavrotas, G., & Chowdhury, A. (2006). FDI and growth: What causes what? *The World Economy, 29*(1), 9–19.

McDonnell, T. (2019, September 17). *Trump froze aid to Guatemala. Now programs are shutting down*. NPR. Retrieved December 4, 2021, from https://www.npr.org/sections/goatsandsoda/2019/09/17/761266169/trump-froze-aid-to-guatemala-now-programs-are-shutting-down

Mearsheimer, J. J. (2018). *The great delusion: Liberal dreams and international realities*. Yale University Press.

Mearsheimer, J. J., & Walt, S. M. (2016). The case for offshore balancing: A superior U.S. grand strategy. *Foreign Affairs*, 70–83.

Mehta, D. (2018, June 19). *Separating families at the border is really unpopular: Even Republicans are split on the issue*. FiveThirtyEight. Retrieved December 5, 2021, from https://fivethirtyeight.com/features/separating-families-at-the-border-is-really-unpopular/

Meyer, J. B. (2008). Network approach versus brain drain: Lessons from the diaspora. *International Migration, 39*(5), 91–110.

Meyer, P. J. (2019). *U.S. strategy for engagement in Central America: Policy issues for congress* (CRS Report). Congressional Research Service.

Meyer, P. J. (2021). *U.S. strategy for engagement in Central America: An overview* (CRS Report). Congressional Research Service.

Morris, S., Rockafellow, R., & Cameron, A. (2022). *Greening the US sovereign bond guarantee program: A proposal to boost climate directed sovereign finance in developing countries* (CGD Policy Paper). Center for Global Development, 1–27.

National Council of Textile Organizations. (2022, January 26). *Independent study highlights benefits of U.S.-CAFTA-DR agreement and devastating impact of weakening agreement's rules*. NCTO. Retrieved January 31, 2022, from https://files.constantcontact.com/8c73c3f4201/ca6406f0-47a3-4693-8b0b-1049490955e5.pdf

National Security Council. (2021). *U.S. strategy for addressing the root causes of migration in Central America*. The White House.

North American Development Bank. (2021). *About NADB*. Retrieved December 1, 2021, from https://www.nadb.org/about/overview

O'Neil, S. K. (2021). *Migrants at the U.S. Border: How Biden's approach differs from Trump's* (Brief). Council on Foreign Relations.

Orihuela, J. C. (2019). The political economy of the developmental state in Latin America. In *Oxford research encyclopedia of politics*. Oxford University Press.

Othering & Belonging Institute. (n.d.). *Climate refugees: Spotlight: The Northern Triangle of Central America (Guatemala, Honduras and El Salvador)*. Othering & Belonging Institute. Retrieved December 12, 2021, from https://belonging.berkeley.edu/climate-refugees-6

Petraeus, D. H., Zoellick, R. B., & O'Neil, S. K. (2014). *North America: Time for a new focus* (Vol. Independent Task Force Report No. 71). Council on Foreign Relations.

Pison, G. (2019). *Population & societies: The number and proportion of immigrants in the population: International comparisons*. French Institute for Demographic Studies, 1–4.

Ravenhill, J. (1998). Cycles of middle power activism: Constraint and choice in Australian and Canadian foreign policies. *Australian Journal of International Affairs, 52*(3), 307–329.

Rieffel, L. (2021, April 30). Normalizing China's relations with the Paris club. Stimson.org. Retrieved December 10, 2021, from https://www.stimson.org/2021/normalizing-chinas-relations-with-the-paris-club/

Rooney, M. (2021). *Central America: Promoting prosperity with targeted U.S. policy* (Policy Brief). George W. Bush Presidential Center.

Runde, D. (2021, March 10). Navigating the United States-Northern Triangle enhanced engagement act. Center for Strategic & International Studies. Retrieved December 1, 2021, from https://www.csis.org/analysis/navigating-united-states-northern-triangle-enhanced-engagement-act

Schnably, S. J. (1994). The Santiago commitment as a call to democracy in the United States: Evaluating the OAS role in Haiti, Peru, and Guatemala. *University of Miami Inter-American Law Review, 25*, 393–453.

Schneider, M. L. (2021, July 21). *Six months on: Changes in U.S. policy toward the Northern Triangle*. Center for Strategic & International Studise. Retrieved December 1, 2021, from https://www.csis.org/analysis/six-months-changes-us-policy-toward-northern-triangle

Scholte, J. A. (2004). Civil society and democratically accountalbe global governance. *Government and Opposition, 39*(2), 211–233.

Schott, J. J., & Goodman, M. P. (2021). *Bringing supply chains back to Mexico: Opportunities and obstacles* (Policy brief). Peterson Institute for International Economics and the Center for Strategic and International Studies.

Sims, J., & Romero, J. (2013, November 22). *Latin American debt crisis of the 1980s*. Federal Reserve History. Retrieved October 30, 2021, from https://www.federalreservehistory.org/essays/latin-american-debt-crisis
Skidmore, T. E., Smith, P. H., & Green, J. N. (2010). *Modern Latin America*. Oxford University Press.
Smith, B. (2008). *Talons of the Eagle: Dynamics of U.S.-Latin American relations* (3rd ed.). Oxford University Press.
Smith, P. H. (2018). The rise and fall of the developmental state in Latin America. In M. Vellinga (Ed.), *The changing role of the state in Latin America* (pp. 51–73). Routledge.
The Economist. (2021, November 13). Biden and the border: Why the situation on America's southern border has become unmanageable. *The Economist*.
Tomasek, R. D. (1959). Defense of the western hemisphere: A need for reexamination of United States policy. *Midwest Journal of Political Science, 3*(4), 374–401.
United Nations. (2021). *Comprehensive development plan for El Salvador, Guatemala, Honduras and south-Southeast Mexico* (United Nations Report). Economic Commission for Latin America.
United States Government Accountability Office. (2021). *The 2019 suspension and reprogramming of U.S. funding adversely affected assistance projects* (GAO Report). United States Government Accountability Office.
U.S. Department of State. (2021, September 16). *U.S. relations with Mexico—Bilateral relations fact sheet*. Retrieved December 1, 2021, from https://www.state.gov/u-s-relations-with-mexico/
U.S. International Development Finance Corporation. (n.d.). *U.S. international development finance corporation*. Who We Are. Retrieved January 25, 2022, from https://www.dfc.gov/who-we-are
Wallace, S. J., & Zepeda-Millán, C. (2020). *Walls, cages, and family separation: Race and immigration policy in the Trump era*. Cambridge University Press.
Walt, S. (2019, March 11). America's polarization is a foreign policy problem, too. *Foreign Policy*. Retrieved December 1, 2021, from https://foreignpolicy.com/2019/03/11/americas-polarization-is-a-foreign-policy-problem-too/
Wilson Center. (2021, November 18). *The 2021 North American leaders summit—Expectations and opportunities*. Wilson Center. Retrieved December 10, 2021, from https://www.wilsoncenter.org/article/2021-north-american-leaders-summit-expectations-and-opportunities
Wise, C. (2020). *Dragonomics: How Latin America is maximizing (or missing out on) China's international development strategy*. Yale University Press.
Yao, Y. (2010). The end of the Beijing consensus: Can China's model of authoritarian growth survive. *Foreign Affairs, 2*, 2–5.
Zakaria, F. (1997). The rise of illiberal democracy. *Foreign Affairs, 76*(6), 22–43.

Zoellick, R. B. (1999). Congress and the making of US foreign policy. *Survival, 41*(4), 20–41.

Zoellick, R. B. (2020). *America in the world: A history of U.S. diplomacy and foreign policy*. Hachette Book Group.

CHAPTER 4

Conclusions and Potential Futures

Abstract The main conclusions and limitations of *Escaping the Governance Trap* are presented. Key limitations include this book's methodology, case selection, focus on economic rather than political reforms, its reticence on the sources of good institutions, and its emphasis on the United States. Several potential futures are then presented, including baseline, downside, and upside scenarios. Trajectories will depend on the balance of power between the Northern Triangle's autonomous states and non-state groups such as transnational criminal organizations, the degree of international support, global economic conditions, and geopolitics. While this list of variables is not exhaustive, it does yield several potential narratives for how the future could unfold for the region and the implications therein. The book closes with a call to action, noting how helping Northern Triangle countries escape their governance traps is critical to regional security and prosperity.

Keywords Governance trap · Northern Triangle economic reform · Scenario analysis of the Northern Triangle

The chapter summarizes *Escaping the Governance Trap's* main conclusions and acknowledges its limitations. It also outlines several potential scenarios for the Northern Triangle based on the evolution of domestic

N. Shenai, *Escaping the Governance Trap*,
https://doi.org/10.1007/978-3-030-99023-7_4

and international variables. Ultimately, the trajectory of the Northern Triangle will be shaped by the willingness of the Northern Triangle populations to demand enhanced governance, the ability of their governments to meet this demand for reform, as well as the degree of support offered by the global community and the international context, including global macroeconomic and political conditions. Strong public demands for accountability and policy entrepreneurs willing to enact reform, along with sustained international support against a backdrop of supportive global conditions, will provide the region the best chance to improve its governance and achieve lasting change.

1 Main Conclusions

This book argued that governance matters for economic performance in the Northern Triangle, and that improving governance can improve the region's prospects. International partners such as the United States, Canada, Mexico, the private sector, civil society, and international financial institutions all have a critical role to play in supporting reform efforts.

This book began by outlining a framework for understanding the economic and political challenges in the Northern Triangle. It argued that the Northern Triangle countries were stuck in a "governance trap," or *path-dependent equilibria in which weak states with contested authority fail to penetrate civil society and achieve self-sustaining economic growth, resulting in states that under supply political order and economic opportunity*. This framework rested on several theoretical propositions, specifically: (i) that the state is an autonomous organization that has a monopoly over the legitimate use of force in a delimited territory and that (ii) weak states have a contested monopoly of force. It provided evidence that the Northern Triangle countries counted as weak states and, as a result, had a mixed ability to provide political order to their territory. Further, (iii) state capacity is a composite of the range of activities it pursues and its coercive ability. Thus, (iv) choosing the appropriate mix of activities and properly calibrating the state's penetration into civil society was critical in promoting high quality governance. In the Northern Triangle, there are some areas where the state's activity should be curtailed, while in other areas its footprint should expand.[1] Strengthening its penetration into civil society would also be beneficial in some areas while detrimental to others. Additionally, (v) state institutions exhibited strongly path-dependent qualities, but (vi) sustained reform efforts stood a chance of helping states move away from path-dependent suboptimal governance outcomes and toward a more responsive and transparent polity over time.

After establishing this governance trap framework and providing some stylized facts regarding the above propositions in the Northern Triangle in chapter one, chapter two of this book turned to economic reforms that could help the Northern Triangle countries escape their governance traps. It focused on how fiscal reform, monetary policy and exchange rate reform, financial reform, and structural reforms can create fiscal space for priority investments and social services, enhance macroeconomic stability, boost financial access while safeguarding the financial system from illicit financial threats, and increase potential gross domestic product growth. It was proposed that these specific reforms were linked in helping the Northern Triangle escape their governance traps by providing mechanisms to strengthen horizontal and vertical accountability while improving the region's economic potential. Some attention was paid to key current topics, including the impact of the COVID-19 pandemic on the Northern Triangle countries and El Salvador's recent adoption of Bitcoin, among others.

Chapter three outlined the role that international allies and partners can play in helping the Northern Triangle countries escape the governance trap. It focused on the United States—historically the most important regional player in the Western Hemisphere—and framed the United States' strategic interests in the Northern Triangle as maintaining regional hegemony, mitigating risks from adverse spillovers including migration, and promoting democratic values and prosperity through free trade and market economies. From these interests followed several principles of engaging the Northern Triangle countries. These principles emphasized the formulation of pragmatic foreign policy, the need to make inter-temporal and strategic compromises, and the benefits of supporting multilateralism to address the Northern Triangle's challenges. The chapter also explained the interests and potential for deeper engagement in the

[1] Chapter two provides specific examples.

Northern Triangle for Canada, Mexico, the private sector, civil society, and international institutions.

2 Limitations of *Escaping the Governance Trap*

There are several limitations of *Escaping the Governance Trap*.

First, *Escaping the Governance Trap* does not employ a formal methodology and research design, advance testable and falsifiable hypotheses, and adhere to a specific disciplinary approach to understand the challenges facing the Northern Triangle countries. As a result, political scientists and economists that are used to studying policy relevant research questions in Central America with this social scientific method may rightly claim that this book fails to meet the logic and evidentiary standards of traditional scholarship. While this is a fair critique, the decision not to present a study with an empirical methodology, which is inherently limiting even with the benefit of rigor, was made consciously. This book attempts to advance a plausible heuristic device of assessing the Northern Triangle's challenges and then outlines an economic reform agenda that can address these challenges. Its goal was not to advance a mutually exclusive explanation for the underdevelopment of the Northern Triangle, nor to prove definitively that governance is a causal, intervening variable that helps explain outbound migration from the Northern Triangle. This book sought to convince the reader that governance deserved serious scrutiny as a causal driver of the region's challenges and that economic reforms had a chance to change the trajectory of the region. It is up to the reader to judge whether they found these arguments persuasive, while subsequent scholarship can analyze the relative merits of the reforms offered in chapter two.

Second, this book does not draw extensively from the experiences of nearby Costa Rica and Panama, both of which had managed to grow their per-capita incomes and address governance vulnerabilities. However, there are several methodological issues in crafting a theoretical and policy relevant agenda by extrapolating from other cases. First, there is an issue of selecting cases on the dependent variable, which implies that one should identify how comparators had similar initial conditions and then studying the drivers of divergences. But it is unclear whether the Northern Triangle countries were truly similarly situated to other cases at a cutoff point, such as 1900, 1945, or 1990. Second, there is a limitation of using inductive reasoning when trying to explain why some countries are rich and others are poor. Third, this book cites other examples of successful reforms in, for example, Northern Mexico, Eastern Europe, and elsewhere, which are relevant to the Northern Triangle countries. Fourth, both Costa Rica and Panama have their own present-day challenges related to governance, including illicit finance vulnerabilities. And both managed to grow their per-capita incomes by drawing on considerable investments in infrastructure, structural reforms, and U.S. public and private sectors' involvement—all of which this book suggests can be applied to the Northern Triangle.[2]

Third, some of the areas of reform studied in chapter two may seem arbitrary to readers—given this book's focus on governance, perhaps it should have focused more on comparative institutional design, public administration, the sociology of political reform, and similar topics. While these are fruitful and complementary areas of inquiry, this book made a conscious decision to focus on *economic reforms* of the major macroeconomic sectors of each country. No discussion of economic reform can occur without considering more traditional political variables, yet successful political reform often depends on complementary economic reform efforts to lock in gains, enhance productivity, and create a stable and growing pool of economic rents to anchor political consensus. The goal of this book is to show that economic reforms can be part of a broader reform agenda in the Northern Triangle, and not to argue that they provide a silver bullet to enhance outcomes and deter outbound migration. That said, economic reforms can be prioritized as they could make it easier to address other policy challenges. For instance, by increasing tax revenue and thus enabling governments to invest more in infrastructure, education, the professionalization of the security services, it could be easier for policy entrepreneurs to extract rents from society and deter tax evasion, thus opening a path for political reform.

Fourth, it could be argued that this book ignored some of the most foundational questions of governance in emerging economies: where do good institutions come from? How should reformers sequence their

[2] For example, see (Gedan, 2016) on how Panama's authorities successfully managed the Panama Canal after handover from the United States. Gedan finds that success is explained by "the determined effort to build a national consensus about the canal's structure and future management," as well as the Panama Canal Authority's legal autonomy. Thus, the political and institutional context of infrastructure management mattered, much as this book has argued. See also (Ferreira, 2009) on Costa Rica's structural reforms.

reforms to maximize their chances of success? What is the appropriate balance between forbearance and conditionality in international support? How can reform be expected in countries when the ruling and business elite benefit materially from the status quo? Again, there are no easy answers to these questions. The advice offered in chapter three, however, sought to show that reform should be patient, sustained, and recognize that strong national ownership is a precondition for success. Creating strong ownership is ultimately a more difficult sociological question than this book can answer, though the answer may emerge from a close study of the interaction among private sector actors, civil society, and international partners, and their ability to demand change while altering the cost–benefit calculus of leaders. Subsequent scholarship can delve into these "big questions," and readers interested in these issues should peruse this book's bibliography.

Fifth, chapter three focuses heavily on the constructive role that the United States can play in the region. Readers may rightly claim that this book has an American bias. Some of this bias is unavoidable, as the author's interest and expertise in the Northern Triangle was shaped during his time in the United States government. Yet it is important to remember that no amount of American energy, be it deployed via rebooted "root causes" initiatives, border security measures, and rhetorical bluster, can substitute for a lack of domestic political will and policy ownership in the Northern Triangle countries themselves. While American action can shape the global context, a far bigger driver of the region's future will be the result of the decisions of individual Salvadorans, Honduras, and Guatemalans. Hopefully, potential reformers read this book and consider it a starting point, and not the final word, of the benefits of economic reforms in the Northern Triangle countries.

3 Scenario Analysis

Having summarized this book's main conclusions and its limitations, the rest of this chapter attempts to peer into the future to speculate on potential trajectories for the region. Scenarios touch upon domestic politics within the Northern Triangle, international support, global conditions, and geopolitical rivalries.[3] While this list of variables is not exhaustive,

[3] As argued by Alina Iancu et al., such a scenario planning approach "are not forecasts or predictions;" rather, they are "narratives that illustrate how an unpredictable future

their evolution will likely play a key role in determining the prospects for reform in the Northern Triangle in the next few decades.

3.1 *The Baseline Scenario: The Status Quo*

In the baseline scenario, the Northern Triangle countries will continue to be stuck in their governance traps. Transnational criminal organizations (TCOs) and organized crime will co-opt the state apparatus for private ends. Vertical and horizontal accountability mechanisms will be established, often due to the pressure of outsiders, but their enforcement power and ability to alter the cost–benefit calculus of policymakers will be limited by domestic political pushback and international ambivalence. Domestic economic policy will blend orthodox approaches, such as inflation targeting, fiscal prudence, and occasional macroeconomic reform, along with extraordinary measures during critical junctures, such as the adoption of Bitcoin or central bank asset purchases. At times, financing needs will require the countries to turn to the international community for support, which will provide episodic windows of opportunity for reform. All three countries will cycle through political leaders disposed toward engaging with the global community and tackling reforms, while at other times catering to the entrenched interests of their power bases, including corporations, TCOs, and oligopolistic economic power centers, while courting new international actors.

International support for enhancing governance reform in the Northern Triangle will be episodic and cyclical. At times, U.S. domestic politics will produce leaders that emphasize punitive measures to deter irregular migration at the Southern border. Policy will lean on immigration enforcement, withdrawn aid, and support from the region, pressure campaigns on third countries to resettle migrants, and the politicization of border security, such as via border wall construction and child separation. Other times, U.S. leadership will emphasize engagement with the region. Policy will target "root causes" of irregular migration as leaders attempt to forge alliances with the private sector and civil society to effect change in the region. Leadership succession in both the United States and in the

might play out… [to] help generate perspectives sufficiently different from those currently held." See (Iancu et al., 2020, p. 25).

Northern Triangle countries will be seen as critical junctures in relationships, with progress and rollbacks depending on sustained political will in both the United States and the Northern Triangle to reform.[4]

Global conditions will improve gradually. The COVID-19 pandemic will eventually recede and become endemic. Restrictions to contain the spread of the virus will be phased out over time. Vaccines will be available globally, while unrestricted trade in viral therapeutics, personal protective equipment, and other material will be forthcoming but with a lag as advanced economies meet the needs of their populations prior to pushing for exports. The climate emergency will continue, though global agreements to reduce emissions have the potential to put a cap on rising temperatures over the medium term. Global macroeconomic conditions will eventually normalize, with extraordinary policy support yielding to more restrictive fiscal and monetary policy in advanced economies. Financial conditions tighten somewhat to their pre-2020 trend, but long-term interest rates remain "lower for longer" in advanced economies, anchoring global capital flows to emerging markets. Support for the liberal trade and monetary system will remain contested, with a gradual shift from *globalism* to *regionalism* as states emphasize supply chain resilience and "just-in-case" manufacturing rather than "just-in-time" global supply chains. These trends could provide a tailwind to the Central American countries when domestic conditions in the United States favor globalization, though its political contestation will remain for the medium term.

Geopolitical rivalry between the United States and China will continue, with diplomacy preventing the emergence of a "hot" conflict between the two powers. Each country will continue to vie for influence and probe the other's capacity to influence outcomes in their near abroad. The United States will strongly emphasize hegemony in the Western Hemisphere as a key foreign policy objective, while its commitments in Asia will be tested by an increasingly assertive China. These incentives will cause leaders in the Northern Triangle to attempt to play China and the United States off one another, in turn reducing the United States' leverage over the region but presenting opportunities to achieve concessions from the great

[4] See (Bernal, 2022) for an example of how the recent election of Xiomara Castro as President of Honduras has been cast by the U.S. media and the White House as an opportunity for deeper engagement. For an additional perspective, see (Narea, 2022).

powers that may have otherwise been unavailable prior to the emergence of China.

3.2 Downside Scenario: Growing Entropy

In a downside scenario, political order in the Northern Triangle countries will deteriorate from current levels, with the balance of power between TCOs and other forms of organized crime and the state tips toward the favor of non-state actors. As a result, more economic activity will take place outside of the purview of the state. TCOs will extract greater rents from the private sector, deterring productive investment. Political leaders, aware that their only path to power is by engaging non-state actors and seeking their support, may fuel a top-down culture of corruption an impunity. Institutional quality will drift, with policy entrepreneurs increasingly prevented from governing. Domestic economic policy further deteriorates with the degradation of technocracy. Policy prudence gives ways to fiscal and monetary largesse. Inflation targets are abandoned, while risks to fiscal and external sustainability grow. Unorthodox policy choices cause the Northern Triangle countries to be locked out of global markets. The rating agencies downgrade debt, currencies depreciate as risk premia rise, and stable finances are put further out of reach. New lenders, aware of the lack of opportunities, step in to fill the void, possibly entrenching pre-existing vulnerabilities. A paralysis of state activity stalls ongoing structural reforms, sapping private sector productivity further.

As a result of the lack of political representation and economic opportunity, migration accelerates. The politics of immigration reform continue to polarize American politics, with the potential for hardline governments gaining popular support for increasingly draconian immigration enforcement policies, including via child separation, greater border infrastructure, harsher penalties for firms that hire irregular migrants, and more proactive search policies on behalf of immigration authorities and law enforcement to root out irregular migrants from society. Family ties among migrant families are strained, hurting the United States' reputation abroad. More aggressive policies further challenge America's liberal values, poisoning the domestic political discourse in the United States and reifying further the toxic political dynamics between the United States and the Northern Triangle governments. Aid flows are permanently curtailed, while the United States seeks to use any available leverage to convince the Northern Triangle countries to take more actions on migration, but with little lasting impact given capacity constraints of the Northern Triangle governments. The United States continues to pressure allies and partners to agree to “safe third country agreements,” further straining its foreign relations.

Global conditions deteriorate. The COVID-19 pandemic continues into the medium term, with the emergence of new, vaccine-resistant variants. Successive waves of the virus continue to threaten to overwhelm the health systems of countries. Political divisions about vaccination and COVID restrictions intensify, straining the domestic politics of leading states and polarizing the health response. Different states defensively guard their intellectual property and engage in protectionism on COVID-19 therapeutics, personal protective equipment, and vaccines. Changing power balances and global discord prevent a consensus on carbon emissions reduction. While some countries commit in principle to a green transition, vested interests that have a stake in the continuation of carbon-intensive growth play spoiler, preventing a reduction in emissions and accelerating the global climate emergency. Extreme weather events occur more regularly and with greater severity, with the poorest and most vulnerable countries such as the Northern Triangle the hardest hit. Global macroeconomic conditions deteriorate amid a sudden rise in global real neutral interest rates and tighter global financial conditions. Emerging markets enter a decade of debt deflation and balance sheet repair, while advanced economies are forced to tighten monetary policy pro-cyclically to contain rising inflation. The Northern Triangle countries find it hard to generate the foreign exchange necessary to meet their maturing external obligations, precipitating debt defaults and protracted macroeconomic adjustment.

Geopolitical rivalry between the United States and China intensifies, with China becoming increasingly militaristic in trying to achieve preeminence in Northeast Asia. After establishing greater regional influence, China attempts to push into the Western Hemisphere, tempting the Northern Triangle countries with promises of investment and additional strategic autonomy should they choose to align with China. China’s push into the Western Hemisphere further inflames tensions between the two great powers, with effects felt in multiple theaters.

3.3 *Upside Scenario: A Renaissance of Cooperation*

In an upside scenario, successive high-profile cases of corruption create backlash against incumbent political and economic elites in the Northern Triangle. The citizens of the Northern Triangle countries demand accountability from their leaders, triggering the election of reform-minded candidates. Broad public mandates for institutional reform create opportunities for the governments of the Northern Triangle to reassert themselves into civil society and to reduce the influence of TCOs and other private actors. Institutional quality steadily improves, with early gains leading to positive feedback in which reformers are rewarded with greater policy latitude to enact further reform. Domestic economic policy helps increase formalization. Tax receipts rise, as a culture of tax compliance takes hold. Fiscal space and resilience are boosted, creating space for priority investments and strengthened social safety nets. Governments are able to offer targeted incentives to firms and households, leading to capital accumulation and boosting per-capita incomes.

International support surges, anchored by strong ownership of reform agendas in the Northern Triangle countries. The United States leads the establishment of semi-permanent anti-impunity missions with broad mandates, complementing domestic accountability mechanisms. The domestic politics surrounding immigration policy in the United States thaws, while the United States' aging population changes the public discourse about migration from deterrence to competition for migrants. The United States creates pathways to citizenship for irregular migrants, boosting labor supply in the United States and ensuring that America's social safety net and public finances remain financially viable in the long term. U.S. leadership no longer fixates on solving the migration problem and instead seeks to work with the Northern Triangle governments on shared challenges. Punitive measures are phased out.

Global conditions continue to improve, anchored by fast technological progress, the green transition, and a renewed global consensus on inclusive growth. The COVID-19 pandemic ends as global herd immunity is achieved. Future virus waves are contained by unrestricted trade in vaccines, therapeutics, and personal protective equipment. Future virus outbreaks are managed through a global early warning system. Bold action on emissions bends the curve on warming global temperatures, reducing the exigency of the climate emergency. Free flowing global capital and technological transfer, as well as novel financing structures, cushion the blow from extreme weather events and help the Northern Triangle countries adapt and mitigate to climate change. Global macroeconomic conditions remain highly favorable to emerging markets. Post-COVID, advanced economies rebuild their policy space as temporary supply disruptions ease. Headline inflation remains anchored by credible central banks. Capital continues to flow toward emerging markets, facilitating consumption smoothing and investment. Support for the liberal trade and monetary system increases, with a thawing in global trade tensions.

Geopolitical rivalry between the United States and China is well managed. The countries continue to probe each other on the margins, but military confrontation is avoided by deterrence and diplomacy. As a result, the Northern Triangle countries are free to establish commercial relationships with myriad international partners. High standards are maintained regardless of creditors. At times, the United States and China will cooperate on shared global challenges, including climate change.

4 Conclusion

The future is unknown, and as of the writing of this book, the global recovery after COVID-19 remains uncertain. It is impossible to probability-weight the above scenarios and arrive at a best estimate of the future trajectories of the Northern Triangle countries. Nevertheless, hopefully the above scenarios illustrated that escaping the governance trap will depend on a strong domestic will to reform, favorable global conditions, and good fortune. Throughout this book, emphasis was placed on the idea that support for long-term strategies could be undermined by their seeming lack of near-term success. Additionally, incorrect presumptions of the existence of good faith reformers willing to undertake reforms consistent with the long-term interests of their populations could breed a cynicism about the prospects of this region. The goal of this book was to show readers that while lasting change is elusive, the right reforms, applied at the right time, by the right leadership, and with the right international support can succeed in helping the Northern Triangle countries escape their governance traps. Ultimately, the future will depend on the political will of the Northern Triangle populations and the willingness of international partners to grasp their outstretched hands.

Works Cited

Bernal, R. (2022, January 28). *Harris bets on new Honduran president to revive Central America policy*. The Hill: https://thehill.com/latino/591745-harris-bets-on-new-honduran-president-to-revive-central-america-policy

Ferreira, G. F. (2009). *The expansion and diversification of the export sector and economic growth: the Costa Rican experience*. LSU Doctoral Dissertations.

Gedan, B. (2016). *Understanding the political economy of successful state-owned enterprise management: A case study of the Panama Canal Authority*. Johns Hopkins University.

Iancu, A., Anderson, G., Ando, S., Boswell, E., Gamba, A., Hakobyan, S., ..., & Wu, Y. (2020). Reserve currenceis in an evolving international monetary system. *International Monetary Fund: Strategy, Policy, & Review Department and Statistics Department Departmental Paper Series, 20*(02), 1–67.

Narea, N. (2022, February 2). *Honduras's new president could help Biden on migration, if she can survive a political crisis*. Vox: https://www.vox.com/policy-and-politics/2022/2/2/22904961/honduras-castro-president-congress-biden-harris-migration

Index

N. Shenai, *Escaping the Governance Trap*,
https://doi.org/10.1007/978-3-030-99023-7

CPSIA information can be obtained
at www.ICGtesting.com
Printed in the USA
LVHW081347090822
725517LV00001B/3

9 783030 990220